Excerpts from
SATAN'S ANGELS EXPOSED

Satan right now is snatching away the Word of God sown in the hearts of the unsaved (Matthew 13:19). He is sowing his counterfeit Christians (the *"tares"*) among the sons of the kingdom (Matthew 13:25, 38, 39) and he is blinding the minds of men to the Gospel (2 Corinthians 4:3-4).   Chapter 1

* * *

The secret organization called **The Illuminati** is an example of the lust of the eyes. They seek power and control and world domination.   Chapter 2

* * *

Nothing sidetracks Satan. He takes no *"coffee breaks."* He sets up imitation churches, imitation ministers, imitation evangelists and imitation Christian music. He is the master of deception.   Chapter 3

* * *

Mohammed did not hold women in high esteem. The Koran speaks of women as man's supreme calamity, and suspects most of them will go to hell.
Chapter 11

* * *

Humanism is just as deadly as witchcraft or communism . . . perhaps even more deadly. Humanism leaders strive to control church nurseries, the use of church buildings and the Christian school curriculum.   Chapter 15

* * *

No witches do not ride on brooms. They are subtle, friendly; some even beautiful and enticing. You may find them at your place of employment, next door, and perhaps even teaching Sunday School (1 Peter 5:8)!   Chapter 16

* * *

A believer in Christ should not be a member of any secret society! This includes Masonic orders.   Chapter 18

* * *

There is a single force that seeks to destroy the world. **The Order of the Illuminati** is one of its servants.   Chapter 19

* * *

The Council on Foreign Relations **(CFR)** has been called *"the invisible government."* Its members have staffed almost every key position of every administration since Franklin D. Roosevelt.   Chapter 25

* * *

All this and much more you will find in the *30 chapters* of this exciting and revealing book that provides you with new information that will make *Satan's Angels Exposed!*

SATAN'S
ANGELS
EXPOSED

by Salem Kirban

Published by SALEM KIRBAN, Inc., Mason's Mill Road, Huntingdon Valley, Pennsylvania 19006. Copyright © 1980 by Salem Kirban. Printed in the United States of America. All rights reserved, including the right to reproduce this book or portions thereof in any form.

Library of Congress Catalog Card No. 80-65329
ISBN 0-912582-32-4

DEDICATION

To **Dr. Gary G. Cohen**
Executive Vice-President
Clearwater Christian College
Clearwater, Florida

It has been my privilege to write 35 books. I have been extremely fortunate in having Dr. Gary G. Cohen carefully proofread each of my books. Because of his scholarly background in Biblical studies, I have been the beneficiary of wise counselling and guidance in my writing. He is always objective, accurate and demonstrates real charity towards others.

Gary's contribution to each book gives added enrichment and is a principal reason for their worldwide acceptance.

I consider it a great honor also to have had the privilege of co-authoring several books with Dr. Cohen including **REVELATION VISUALIZED** and **The Salem Kirban REFERENCE BIBLE.**

Dr. Cohen is the author of:

The Horsemen Are Coming (prophecy novel), Moody Press, 1979.
Understanding Revelation, Moody Press, 1979.
Weep Not For Me (on the Fall of Jerusalem, 70 A.D.), Moody Press, 1980.
Amos-Hosea: Everyman's Bible Commentary, Moody Press, 1980.
Biblical Separation Defended, Presbyterian & Reformed, Nutley, N.J., 1966.
Pilgrim's Progress In the 20th Century, 1968, 3400 Gulf-to-Bay, Clearwater, Florida 33515, $2.50.

I highly recommend you read his books.

ACKNOWLEDGMENTS

To **Dr. Gary G. Cohen,** Executive Vice President at Clearwater Christian College, Clearwater, Florida, who carefully checked the final manuscript.

To **Doreen Frick,** who devoted many hours proofreading the text.

To **Batsch Company,** for excellent craftsmanship in setting the type.

To **Walter W. Slotilock,** Chapel Hill Litho, for negatives.

To **Koechel Designs,** for an excellent cover design.

To **Dickinson Brothers, Inc.,** for printing this book.

CONTENTS

WHY I WROTE THIS BOOK

This is not a book that I wanted to write. The Lord burdened my heart to write this book in October, 1978. But I kept on putting it off, not writing it until 14 months later!

I would have much preferred spending my time writing a book on triumphant Christian living. I came to realize, however, that much of the Bible deals with Satan, his program and his final destiny. Yet few Bible believers are really aware who Satan is and how he operates.

The world's idea of Satan is someone with a pitchfork and long tail with an evil expression on his face. Many Christians, unfortunately, have this same conception of Satan. Most are unaware that Satan has multitudes of fallen angels who do his bidding. These demon angels not only work in ordinary realms but are very active in the political and religious realms.

<u>Satan is not dead!</u> Nor does he always appear as obviously evil. As this age draws to a close, Satan is becoming once again very active in entering human bodies and controlling personalities. He is a subtle deceiver who could be achieving his aims through an entertaining television star, even through a religious musical group or an unbelieving Sunday School teacher!

Satan would have believers enter into the hysteria of the day accusing fellow believers, causing divisions in churches and spending more time studying Satan, the Illuminati or Witchcraft . . . while the Atheists and Communists take half the world.

Remember, Satan is already a defeated foe! As believers, we should appropriate God's way for victory (Ephesians 6:10-20; James 4:7,8). It is my prayer that this book will change your life . . . now that you have seen Satan's angels exposed!

Salem Kirban

Huntingdon Valley, Pennsylvania
U.S.A., January, 1980

1

SATAN'S ANGELS EXPOSED

**Satan's
Subtle
Deception
Now in
The
Church**

If we are to be victorious in the warfare against Satan, it is important that we know the tactics of the one with whom we are at war! It is important to realize that Satan works through men. He works at times through governmental leaders, through organizations ... yes, even through the Church!

Satan was originally known by the name of **Lucifer.** Lucifer means "*the light bearer*" or "*the brilliant one.*" Lucifer was a created being (Ezekiel 28:15). The Bible tells us "*Thou (Satan) wast perfect in thy ways ...*" (Ezekiel 28:15).

And not only was Lucifer perfect but he was also "*full of wisdom and perfect in beauty*" (Ezekiel 28:12). Lucifer seems to have been an archangel, perhaps the administrator over the angelic realm. Because Lucifer had the ability to choose, he wanted to ascend from his exalted position even higher into a position of equality with God. This may have involved an attempted move from the second heaven of interstellar space into the *abode of God (the third heaven)*.

When Lucifer rebelled against God in the Heavens, he then became **Satan**. No longer an angel of light, his name . . . Satan . . . means *adversary, to lie in wait, to oppose*. He is also called *Beelzebub* (Matthew 12:24), *the prince of devils* (Matthew 4:1), *Belial* (2 Corinthians 6:15), and *the great dragon* (Revelation 12:9).

In Satan's original rebellion against God it is revealed that ". . . *his tail* (Satan) *swept away a third of the stars of heaven . . .*" (Revelation 12:4). Think of this for a moment: 1/3rd of the angels in heaven followed Satan! These fallen angels who became Satan's army have apparently retained much or all of the power, and all the wisdom that they had before the fall! They are now, as fallen angels, called **demons!**

Satan's Powers Are Vast . . .

Satan is not omnipresent. However, he has a vast army of angels, fallen angels (demons) and they are not limited by time nor space! They work for Satan 24 hours a day. They take no coffee breaks nor vacations! The Apostle Paul pictures Satan as a "roaring lion."

Satan exercises authority in two realms:

1. **The heavenlies**
   As "*the prince of the power of the air*"
   (Ephesians 2:2) he skillfully directs an
   organized host of wicked spirits. Paul
   reminds us: "*. . . our struggle is not
   against flesh and blood, but against . . .
   the powers, against the world forces of
   this darkness, against the spiritual
   forces of wickedness in the heavenly
   places* (Ephesians 6:12).

2. **This world**
   This present world is in the grip of and
   passively yielded to the power of Satan.
   Numerous verses tell us that Satan is
   "*. . . the prince of this world*" (John
   12:31; 14:30; 16:11) . . . and also of this
   evil world-system which he has organized upon his own principles (2 Corinthians 4:3-4).

Satan right now is snatching away the
Word of God sown in the hearts of the
unsaved (Matthew 13:19), he is sowing his
counterfeit Christians (the "*tares*") among
the sons of the kingdom (Matthew 13:25,
38-39) and he is blinding the minds of men
to the Gospel (2 Corinthians 4:3-4).

**Satan's
Angels
Present
Today**

Angels do not have a limited life span as
humans do. Angels do not die. Every angel
created still lives today!

The fallen angels who follow Satan are referred to as demons. And the Scriptures
tell us that these demon angels are innumerable.

Because Satan is the prince of this world,
his legions of angels surround us. Ac-

Both Adam and Eve were swayed by Satan's subtle seduction. Because of their sin, they had to leave the Garden of Eden.

tually, we are facing a foe we cannot see! While we cannot see these demons, we can witness the effect they are having on world conditions and on human beings.

Satan's Clever Deception

Satan's body was made for heavenly existence. Unlike the Lord God, Satan cannot materialize his body to appear in earthly form. Instead he has to control and appropriate someone else's body.

In tempting Eve, he used the body of a serpent.

Satan is a deceiver. He is a master of the lie. In order for him to achieve his goals he uses clever deception. He so deceived the Pharisees that they looked at Jesus Christ as their enemy, not their Saviour. And Christ said to them:

> *You are of your father the devil,*
> *and you want to do*
> *the desires of your father.*
> *He (Satan) was a murderer from the*
>   *beginning. And does not stand in the*
>   *truth, because there is no truth in him.*
> *Whenever he speaks a lie,*
>   *he speaks from his own nature;*
>   *for he is a liar,*
>   *and the father of lies*
> *But because I speak the truth,*
>   *you do not believe Me.*
>
> (John 8:44-45)

You can see how clever and effective Satan is. He so deludes those who follow him that they will not believe truth, but rather would choose to believe a lie. Thus through deceit humans become entrapped in the web of Satanic influence.

Does not this bring to mind the verse relating to the Tribulation Period where we are told:

> And for this cause
> God shall send them strong delusion,
> that they should believe a lie.
>
> (2 Thessalonians 2:11)

Perhaps Satan's biggest band of demon angels is engaged constantly in the subtle battle to convey that the Bible is not the Word of God? Satan certainly has had some measure of success in this campaign. The Bible reveals:

> . . . the Spirit speaketh expressly that,
> in the latter times,
> some shall depart from the faith,
> giving heed to seducing spirits,
> and doctrines of demons.
>
> (1 Timothy 4:1)

Dr. J. Vernon McGee's observation is that ". . . they will depart from the faith not because of intellectual or scientific knowledge. There is a return to the spirit world."

Satan In The Church

But, particularly in these Last Days, we must be very discerning Christians, not swayed by every popular religious program. God warns us:

> Beware of false prophets,
> who come to you in sheep's clothing,
> but inwardly
> they are ravening wolves.
> Ye shall know them by their fruits.
>
> (Matthew 6:15-16)

More will be said about this later. But today we may be witnessing the gradual infiltration of Satanic influence into the Christian church. Some "*Christian*" leaders may be like the Pharisees, servants of Satan. God must be the final Judge.

Because some who name the name of Christ appear to be highly successful, we have a tendency to compromise the Gospel when they ignore certain basic Scriptural doctrines including those of separation from unbelievers and evil associations.

Therefore, Paul warns us that in these Last Days, some believers will be fooled by teachers who will take them away from the truth and pollute them with doctrines that are propagated by the devil. He reminds us that Satan will dominate the religious realm so that what we may hear in the name of Christianity actually bears no resemblance to Biblical Christianity. An excellent book to read on this subject is <u>Your Adversary, The Devil</u> by J. Dwight Pentecost.

2

SATAN, THE GREAT IMITATOR

**Satan
Will
Be
Successful**

As we know, during the Tribulation Period, Satan working through Antichrist and the False Prophet will imitate the attributes of God. And, for a time, he will be successful. He will imitate God through miracles, through acting as a peacemaker, through a false, seducing religion.

Today, Satan imitates God:

1. **Through imitation Churches**
   Some even testify that they were initiated into witchcraft by a Sunday School teacher.

2. **Through music**
   Satan destroys the testimony of young Christians by wooing them through music that appears to be Christian but is actually Satanically inspired and controlled.

3. **Through outreach ministries**
   Because there are some seemingly effective evangelical ministries that are reaching around the world, Satan has introduced his imitation evangelism that appears to some to be of Christ, but, by their fruits, indicate they are controlled by Satan's demon angels.

Paul summarizes this deception pointedly when he says:

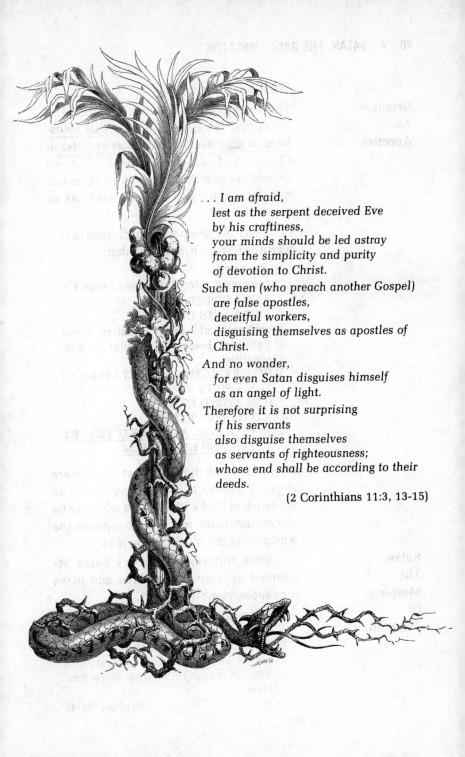

... I am afraid,
lest as the serpent deceived Eve
by his craftiness,
your minds should be led astray
from the simplicity and purity
of devotion to Christ.

Such men (who preach another Gospel)
are false apostles,
deceitful workers,
disguising themselves as apostles of
Christ.

And no wonder,
for even Satan disguises himself
as an angel of light.

Therefore it is not surprising
if his servants
also disguise themselves
as servants of righteousness;
whose end shall be according to their
deeds.

(2 Corinthians 11:3, 13-15)

What does this reveal?

**Disguised
As
Apostles**

These verses tell us that men, controlled by Satan and his demon angels, **will transform or disguise themselves as apostles of Christ.** And we are reminded, that we should not be surprised for even Satan has transformed himself into a disguise as an angel of light!

Can you fully grasp the significance of this warning? What it means is that:

EVEN TODAY
THERE ARE THOSE WHO WE LOOK ON
   AND RESPECT
AS SERVANTS OF CHRIST . . .
World political leaders, Ministers, World
   Religious leaders, TV religious per-
   sonalities
WHO ARE ACTUALLY IMITATORS IN
   THEIR PIETY
FALSE APOSTLES
DECEITFUL WORKERS
CONTROLLED AND DIRECTED BY
   SATAN AND HIS ANGELS!

How important, therefore, that we measure every Christian witness against the yardstick of God's Word. This will give us discernment and enable us to separate the wheat from the chaff (1 John 4:1).

**Satan
The
Master
Of
Temptation**

On three different occasions Satan attempted to tempt Jesus Christ and make him subservient to himself.

1. **In the wilderness**—to have His physical needs met!
   After Christ had fasted 40 days and 40 nights and then became hungry . . . Satan challenged him to turn stones into bread.

   (Matthew 4:1-4)

2. **On the pinnacle**—to have Him doubt the proof of God's presence with Him! Satan placed Jesus Christ on the pinnacle of the Temple in Jerusalem; some 400 feet high and challenged him to jump off.

(Matthew 4:5-7)

3. **On a very high mountain**—to have Him desire the fulfillment of God's promises IMMEDIATELY!
Satan took Jesus Christ to a very high mountain and showed him all the kingdoms of the world, pointing out their glory. Satan offered to give Christ this complete earthly kingdom. All Christ had to do was to kneel down and worship Satan.

(Matthew 4:8-11)

Satan Uses The Bible

In each of these attempts to tempt Jesus Christ, Satan, the Master Deceiver, failed!

No doubt this infuriated Satan. And from that day forward he perhaps increased, with evangelistic fervor, his plan to deceive the world.

Today, it appears more than ever before, Satan and his fallen angels are becoming more and more successful in their demonic activity not only with godless people but even with those who appear to be godly.

Satan attempted to deceive Christ by using the Word of God by reminding Christ:

for it is written,
    HE WILL GIVE HIS ANGELS CHARGE
    CONCERNING YOU . . .

(Matthew 4:6)

When Satan showed Jesus Christ the entire earthly kingdom and promised that it all

Satan on three different occasions attempted to tempt Jesus Christ and make Christ subservient to himself (Matthew 4:1-11)!

could be His if He worshipped Satan, he was appealing to the lust of the eyes . . . the desire for power.

The lust of the flesh, the lust of the eyes, the pride of life . . . all are tools used by Satan today to win converts to his army.

The secret organization called **The Illuminati** is an example of the lust of the eyes. They seek power and control and world domination. They have become tools of Satan. They viewed the earthly kingdom and coveted it.

3

SATAN'S METHOD OF OPERATION

Satan
Is
Not
Lazy!

Satan runs a very efficient organization. He operates a *"tight ship."* He is not lazy . . . nor are his demon angels. He does not waste his time heaping pleasures and luxuries on himself. His devotion is singular . . . that of winning his converts and controlling the world. And nothing sidetracks him . . . nothing!

When he can't make inroads into the Christian church . . . he sets up imitation churches, imitation ministers, imitation evangelists, imitation Christian music. This is his trump card. He is a master of deception. He is the wolf in sheep's clothing (Matthew 7:15).

Just as God has a hierarchy (a power structure) so also has Satan. All the fallen angels may even have individually assigned responsibilities. Their over-all responsibility is to defeat God's program.

We are told in Revelation 9:11 that during the Tribulation Period at the Fifth Trumpet judgment the bottomless pit is opened and innumerable demons are released whose task is to inflict torture and suffering upon the world population. The king of these demons (possibly Satan) is called

Abaddon (in Hebrew)
Apollyon (in Greek)

It means "one who exterminates or destroys." They will not be permitted to touch those who God has sealed (Revelation 9:4).

Satan Blinds Christians

One of Satan's most effective methods of operation is to blind Christians into believing that there are no demons. It is odd that people will believe that angels exist but refuse to believe that demons not only exist but are active right now . . . today!

Demons work actively today both in the political and religious realm! Demons were active in the religious realm even in the days of Moses when the Israelites were going through a religious ritual that outwardly appeared as worship. Moses commanded:

They shall no longer
sacrifice their sacrifices
to the goat-demons [Hebrews: Soerim]
with which they play the harlot . . .
(Leviticus 17:7)

Satan's Aides

Because demons do not possess a body of flesh and blood it is necessary to manifest their presence through people. They must possess or control either the body of an animal or the body of an individual.

Demons show their power by controlling:

1. The mind (Matthew 17:15)
2. The body (Matthew 9:32-33)
3. The emotions (Luke 8:26-39)

Those who have not accepted Jesus Christ as their Saviour and Lord can be controlled by demons. The unsaved, actually are part of Satan's kingdom. They submit to his authority, with little resistance. They are controlled by his angelic demons. Now can you understand why this world is not getting better and how deception has even crept into the Church? It is because all the unsaved are Satan's unwitting Robots and sometimes his willing Ambassadors . . . engineered and programmed to follow his directions and to accomplish his aims of denying the saving power of the Word of God and of polluting and watering down Christian testimony to destroy its effectiveness. Satan will accomplish this through governments, through world leaders, through political leaders, through religious leaders masquerading as angels of light!

Believers Can Be Controlled By Satan

While the unsaved can be controlled by every whim of Satan, believers can be influenced only by the consent of their own will. Because the believer is subject to the authority of Christ, Christ prevents the believer to allow himself to become influenced by Satan or a demon . . . to a point where the believer may become a troublemaker both to himself and to the church.

All Illness Not Of Satan

Of course, too many Christians are attributing every problem, every illness to Satan and his demons. This is wrong. As an example, they will eat junk foods all their life, top it off daily with sweet desserts, chocolate cake, etc. Then they get sick and attribute the illness to demons.

Or they will be on the run daily, serving on every possible church committee, active in church socials and fellowship dinners . . . running, running, running, never taking time to "rest in the Lord." Mark 6:31, "Come ye . . . rest a while," is a passage of Scripture that all busy people (particularly Pastors) should follow diligently. How many do you know that are always busy, always running. Then suddenly they suffer a nervous breakdown or emotional imbalance. Their marriage falls apart. Their children become wayward and perhaps go on drugs. How quick they are to blame it on Satanic demons. (I received several paper cuts while typing this section. I could have attributed it to demons . . . but quite honestly it was due to my own carelessness.)

The Believer's Authority Over Satan And Demons

Yes, believers can be influenced, and perhaps even controlled by Satan. Nevertheless, we must beware of the hysteria that attributes every misadventure to Satan. And some churches are promoting this theology because it keeps the congregation subservient to them.

Satan cult death?

Teacher may have been sexually assaulted, tortured before she was slain, probers say

Weird Cults—From Witches to Satan Worshipers—Infiltrating U.S. Army

So many wacky cults, ranging from witches to Satan worshipers, are infiltrating the U.S. Army that chaplains have been issued a handbook to help them understand and deal with these far-out groups.

Satan-worship cults said to be growing in U.S.

Traces of the Occult on a Farm Pose Mystery for Arkansas Town

By JOHN M. CREWDSON

Special to The New York Times

BENTONVILLE, Ark, June 27—Steve Ferguson was hauling rocks off old Doc Compton's farm on the outskirts of town when he spotted what looked like some kind of altar, native fieldstones piled one upon the other, peeking through the briar and bramble amid the hickory and sycamore trees.

Mr. Ferguson took a closer look, then ran to call the landlord, Dr. Neil Compton. Together, the two men stood and stared at the discovery. "It was built up like a fireplace would be," Dr. Compton recalled. "In the center was the skull."

in addition to a plastic human skull, some candles, a large knife and more of the peculiar symbols, someone had left a message scrawled in painted white letters: "Zyto's wrath is upon you."

"Steve wrote a little note back to them," Dr. Compton said, "and said, 'The power of The Lord is greater.' Steve's a very religious fellow."

After examining the second batch of rocks, Sergeant Green said, he thought he had an idea of what was going on. On a hunch, he asked a bookstore in town to get him a book on witchcraft and demonology.

When it arrived, he found that it

Satan Lives!

So Say Believers Who Call Him God

By Daniel St. Albin Greene

Satan fears the power of God. And, as believers, we can call on this power. We are told:

> Submit therefore to God.
>   Resist the devil
>   and he will flee from you.
>
> (James 4:7)

Paul, grieved over a woman possessed of a demon, said:

> . . . I command you in the name of Jesus Christ to come out . . .
> And it (the demon) came out at that very moment.
>
> (Acts 16:18)

You may recall in Mark 1:23-27, Jesus met a man in the synagogue who was possessed by a demon.

Think of it . . . right there in the Capernaum church or synagogue there were demons! Jesus rebuked the demon and commanded him to come out of the man.

Now the demon recognized Christ for he said:

> What do we have to do with You,
>   Jesus of Nazareth?
> Have you come to destroy us?
> I know who You are—the Holy One of
>   God!
>
> (Mark 1:24)

You see, even the demons recognize Christ when they meet Him. They believe that He exists. Can you now see how foolish every man or woman is today who does not believe that God exists! If Satan and the demons believe (and they came from Heaven) no wonder they can control man who doesn't even have enough discernment to believe that God does exist!

How To Extinguish Satan's Influence

Not only do the demons believe . . . but they are fearful of the power of God . . . for they know He has absolute authority over them. Therefore, because believers are united with God . . . they through God's power can share the benefits of Christ's authority over Satan and his angel demons! God gave His Son, Jesus Christ, power over the angelic realm and over the realm of Satan . . . and because we are in Christ Jesus, we also have this authority!

Can you recognize this fact? Then apply it to your heart . . . and exercise it whenever the devil's angels seek to make inroads in your life! If you actively oppose Satan, in the name of the Lord, Satan will flee from you. This is Scriptural. Read James 4:7 and 1 Peter 5:9. Ephesians 6:13 reminds us that if we put on the whole armor of God we will be able to stand against or resist the power of Satan in this evil day.

Don't Be A Defeated Christian!

I remember attending a missionary conference at Prairie Bible Institute in April, 1977. A student, with tears in his eyes and crying, told how all his life he remembered his mother living the life of a defeated Christian until one day she committed suicide. He sobbed: "I don't want to live the life of a defeated Christian!"

God did not save us and bring us into His family to live a life of defeat. We should not tremble at the wiles of the devil . . . or the adverse circumstances that sometimes surround us.

Christ was and is victorious over Satan. And because we are His, we, too, share in this same daily victory! Defeat? NEVER! We are on the victory side. Satan knows it! And it gives him a migraine headache. No, he doesn't take two Bufferin. He gets rid of his migraine by fooling two more Christians (so to speak) into becoming DEFEATED CHRISTIANS!

Resist the devil. Align yourself with Christ's invincible power. Satan and his demons will flee from you. It's Scriptural ... and God cannot lie! Appropriate the promise every day, every hour, every minute!

4

SATAN'S AMBASSADORS
DOWN THE CORRIDORS OF TIME

Satan's Strategy

Now that you realize that as a believer, through Christ, you have power over Satan and his fallen angelic demons ... let us, without fear, examine Satan's strategy over the years working through individuals.

Christians should not constantly dwell on Satan and his activities but the Bible does direct us to:

> ... be as wise (or shrewd) as serpents and harmless (or innocent) as doves.
>
> (Matthew 10:16)

It is hoped that the succeeding pages will give you wisdom as to the battle plan of Satan so you can avoid deception. May it also help you warn and alert fellow believers (as well as those to whom you are witnessing) of those posing as angels of light but whose Master is Satan!

Satan's invisible army is an army of demons. Demons have distinct personalities. They are invisible individuals.

The word "demon," in the Greek, comes

from an adjective meaning *"intelligent"* or *"knowing."*

Demons possess <u>unusual strength</u>. Remember in Mark 5:9 when the Gadarene demoniac was dominated by a legion of demons. A Roman legion consisted of some 5000 foot soldiers. Then, when the Lord ordered the demons into 2000 swine, they rushed headlong into the sea and destroyed themselves.

Gifts Of Healing

As the great imitator Satan also enters the realm of employing the *"gifts of healing."* We are witnessing a rash of healing ministries in the United States and worldwide. Most are financially successful and reach vast audiences. Their emphasis is on healing. Some of these ministries are of God; others are of Satan, posing as angels of light. God's people should not be so naïve to believe that all healings are of God. Be wise as serpents.

God's Word reminds us:

> Not everyone who says to Me,
>   Lord, Lord,
> will enter the kingdom of heaven;
> but he who does the will of my Father
> who is in heaven.

> Many will say to Me on that day,
>   Lord, Lord,
>   did we not prophesy in Your name,
>   and in Your name cast out demons,
>   and in Your name perform many
>   miracles?

> And then I will declare to them,
> I never knew you:
> DEPART FROM ME . . .
>   (Matthew 7:22-23)

Dr. Merrill F. Unger in Demons in the World Today, writes:

> To claim healing "in the name of the Lord" simply means that it is done through the power of Christ . . .
>
> Magic charmers lay great stress upon the efficiency of the magic word, since it is considered a power in itself. But when the magic healer uses God's name and Bible words, they no longer stand for God.
>
> The word itself is idolized and the creature is set up against the Creator. But the word isolated from God and the clear directives of the Scripture falls a prey to demonic power. This is certainly true of unsaved healing practicioners who use the veneer of Christian profession to cloak their magic technique. . . .[1]

Not Always Of God

Healing is not always an evidence of God's power nor God's blessing on a ministry. Can you grasp the significance of this statement?

Some were healed in pagan temples in the temple of Serapis at Alexandria, Egypt. Demon-directed healers were successful in the days of the early Christians. See Acts 8:9-11 and 13:7-10.

Paul reminds us:

> In the last days
> perilous times shall come.
>
> For men shall be
> lovers of their own selves . . .
> Having a form of godliness,
> but denying the power of it . . .
>
> (2 Timothy 3:1, 2, 5)

---

[1] Merrill F. Unger, Demons in the World Today (Illinois: Tyndale House Publishers, 1971), pp. 126-127.

Satan knows how gullible people are . . . particularly when they fall ill and seek "*immediate*" healing. That is why his demons are ever ready to win another convert via the "*healing*" route. It is one of the easiest avenues for success he can rely on!

One of the evidences of the End Times in which we now live is a rise in the occult. We are seeing a rise in multiple ministries . . . many of which have a form of godliness but their power is from Satan.

They are Satan's Ambassadors!

Where Are Demons Active?

In the book of Deuteronomy (Old Testament) God reveals through Moses what areas the people of Israel should avoid. He lists these demon activities. There are **nine** of them that are Satanic. See Deuteronomy 18:10-11.

1. Anyone who makes his son or his daughter pass through the fire
   The Canaanites offered their children as human sacrifices to their deities.

Healing was part of the ministry of Jesus Christ.

The Lord used a talking donkey to get Balaam's attention.

2. Anyone who uses divination
   Foretelling the future by magical means. Laban claimed to have this power (Genesis 30:27) as did Balaam (Numbers 23:23). Sacrificing animals and *"reading"* their liver to determine a course of action was routine for Roman military procedures.

3. Anyone who practices witchcraft
   This refers to consulting with someone via astrology or certain signs.

4. Anyone who interprets omens
   One who interprets omens is an enchanter, who is under demonic control and brings another another demonic control by his casting of a spell. This is similar to today's witchcraft.

5. Anyone who is a sorcerer
   Sorcery is a general term which would incorporate witchcraft, the use of occult formulas, mystic mutterings, incantations.

6. Anyone who casts a spell
   A charmer who casts a spell is a sorcerer who performs supernatural feats.

7. Anyone who is a medium
   This is one who consults with familiar spirits.

8. Anyone who is a spiritist or wizard
   A wizard is a male medium who receives superhuman knowledge through his contacts with demons.

9. Anyone who calls up the dead
   This is one who has gained his information from departed ones.

God counts these as *"an abomination unto the Lord"* (Deuteronomy 18:12). These demonic activities are still practiced today . . . perhaps with even greater fervency.

5

HOW TO SPOT A FALSE RELIGION

**Satan
Master
Of
Deception**

Satan is not so foolish that he publishes his battle plan to control the world. He is the master of deception.

Naturally we can see some things that are obviously satanically inspired . . . liquor, drugs, crimes. It may, however, be very difficult for you to imagine that Satan's most effective battleground may be right within the church.

What are some basic patterns that we can look at that will give us some idea as to how to judge whether a group of people or an organization is of Satan or of God?

**The
Love
Of
Money**

First, God's Word does tell us that:

> . . . the love of money
> is the root of all evil.

(1 Timothy 6:10)

Thus, we can determine that all manner of evil starts with the love of money. Money, in itself, is not important. The important aspect of money is its POWER TO CONTROL. Notice that this verse does NOT say that money is the root of all evil. Money is not evil. The **love** of it is.

If you look down the pages of history you will see those who were obviously satanically inspired had a lust for power . . . power that came about by seeking after money. It became an overpowering obsession with wealth. What singular attribute is recognizable among all the major cults of today? Their wealth . . . a lust for wealth . . . a love for money. You see their followers willing to take on poverty, to sell trinkets in airport terminals . . . so their leader can accumulate wealth. This wealth . . . this love for money, is turned into impressive buildings . . . the purchases of large businesses.

Thus the love for money brings wealth. Wealth brings accumulation of assets. Accumulation of assets brings power. Power brings control. Control brings subservience of others under this power and allegiance to this power.

**By
Their
Fruits**

Second, you can tell a false prophet and a false religion by their fruits! Any discerning Christian can quickly spot a false prophet. God's Word tells us:

*Beware of false prophets,
which come to you in sheep's clothing,
but inwardly are ravening wolves.*

*Ye shall know them by their fruits.
A good tree cannot bring forth evil fruit,
neither can a corrupt tree
bring forth good fruit.
Wherefore, by their fruits
ye shall know them.*

(Matthew 7:15,16,18,19)

Look at some of your major cults of today. Look at their fruits. They employ brain washing, they strive for secrecy, they turn

Saturday night, November 18, 1978, self-styled Messiah, Jim Jones, led hundreds of followers in Jonestown, Guyana, in a suicide cult of death. Men, women and children drank a strawberry Flavour-aide that was mixed with painkillers, tranquilizers and cyanide. Initial reports indicated that some 300 had committed suicide. But when U.S. soldiers finally tallied the stacks of bodies piled atop each other at the campsite, the total count soared over 900! Jones, a false prophet, headed the People's Temple in San Francisco. It was reported assets turned over to him by his followers totaled over $7 Million.

This tragedy equalled the mass suicide of Jewish Zealots who defended the fortress of Masada against besieging Roman legions in 73 A.D. Here 960 men, women and children died in self-slaughter; however, for a righteous cause. Events such as the Jonestown cult suicide may eventually cause a backlash against any faith that is not within the "conventional, organized religions" of denominations in the World Council of Churches. This will bring on persecution of Bible believers and the rise of the False Prophet during the Tribulation Period.

out computerized people whose values have been warped and whose will has been broken. They attempt to hide their satanic influence by doing good deeds or appearing godly. In many cases they skillfully try to blend Scripture with their own carefully worded theologies. Jehovah's Witnesses and Armstrong's Worldwide Church of God has led many astray in this way.

New Revelations

Third, you can spot a false prophet or false religion because they always add or subtract from God's Word! Even in Paul's day, many of the Galatians who had heard the Gospel were turning away from Christ and following a different way which they thought would lead to Heaven. Paul warns them that the way they are following will not lead to Heaven at all:

> I marvel that ye are so soon removed
> from Him that called you
> into the grace of Christ
> unto another gospel:
> Which is not another;
> but there be some that trouble you,
> and would pervert the Gospel of Christ.
> But though we,
> or an angel from Heaven,
> preach any other gospel unto you
> than that which we have preached unto
> you, let him be accursed.
>
> (Galatians 1:6-8)

These are strong, clear words from Paul. *"Let him be accursed"* means *"Let him be doomed to eternal punishment."* And to make sure there is no misunderstanding,

Paul repeats himself in the very next verse:

> As we said before,
> so say I now again,
> If any man
> preach any other gospel unto you,
> than that ye have received,
> let him be accursed.

(Galatians 1:9)

Other Gospels

What are these other "gospels" that we are to judge on this basis? Gospel means "good news." Too often we think this pertains simply to other religious groups or cults. It is easy for us to say that Hare Krishna, The Unification Church, British-Israelism or Armstrongism are obviously "other gospels" and therefore false.

But other gospels include such things as Transcendental Meditation (TM), mind control groups like EST, some holistic health groups, yoga. They also include some business conglomerates whose basic motives are evil. They include some political groups and political alliances. They also include some church groups.

As I said at the beginning of this chapter, Satan does not publish his battle plans and his allies. His comrades know each other. They have secret signs, secret symbols . . . for birds of a feather flock together. But Satan's strategy thrives on secrecy, surprise, suspense.

But as you examine other religions in particular it is very easy to see that they either ADD or SUBTRACT from the Bible. The usual approach is that

Yes, we believe the Bible.
We even believe in Jesus Christ.

Then they go on to tell you that a <u>later</u> <u>prophet</u> after Christ has come or a <u>later</u> <u>revelation</u>. If you are not familiar with God's Word you can very easily be trapped into Satan's web of deception.

Beware Of Emotionalism

<u>Don't allow your belief in Christ to be governed solely by emotion!</u> I cannot overemphasize this. I repeat, don't allow your belief in Christ to be governed solely by emotion! Emotion must be channeled by the river banks of DOCTRINE. A river with no banks is a swamp. Too many believers today are not firmly stationed on the Solid Rock but rest precariously on the shifting sand of emotion. Is it any wonder that they are swept away so easily by one of Satan's messengers.

It must be remembered that Satan is a defeated foe. His destiny has already been determined by God, and the destiny of his followers will also be judged at the Great White Throne Judgment. In the meantime, Satan and his followers will try to swallow up as many gullible individuals as he can. Don't allow yourself to become caught in his web.

Arm Yourself With The Word Of God

In your own effort, you cannot outsmart Satan! There is only one thing that makes him tremble . . . the word of God.

Satan trembles when he sees
The vilest sinner on his knees!

Remember, you will not be able to look at

any organization or business or political group and say "That is governed by Satan!" The mode of operation is so secretive that few are obviously satanic by their outward public image.

Remember this, however, you can make good headway by sizing up any questionable group with this measuring rod:

1. Do they have a love for money?
2. Has that love for money given them power?
3. What are their fruits?
4. Do they add or subtract from God's Word, the Bible?

Don't be guilty of preaching "*another gospel*," or striving to win someone to another gospel. The fruit of continuing in this is eternal punishment in Hell (Galatians 1:9).

If you become grounded in the Word of God, the lightning bolts of Satan will scatter harmlessly around you!

6

BATTLE OVER BABYLON

Satan's Sensual Beginnings

From the very beginning of time Satan blinded men and caused them to perform the most degrading forms of idolatry.

Satan's army of angels swarmed around the world . . . and were actively successful even before the time of Abraham. Various forms of demonology, like a deadly venom, engulfed the cultures of Sumeria, Babylon, Egypt, Assyria, Chaldeans, Greek and Roman antiquity. It spread to India, China, Japan . . . to Africa and to South America.

Perhaps its strongest influence is felt right now in the United States where, like a hurricane, its full fury is engulfing every strata of society and even seeping into the Christian church.

The Fruits Of Sin

Paul, in Romans, lists the fruits of those who because of their unbelief, suppress the truth. He warns:

> . . . even though they knew God,
>   they did not honor Him as God . . .
> Professing to be wise,
>   they became fools,
> And exchanged
>   the glory of the incorruptible God
>   for an image
>   in the form of corruptible man
>   and of birds and four-footed animals
>   and crawling creatures.

And because they did not honor God nor give thanks for His creation:

Therefore God gave them over
in the lusts of their hearts
to impurity,
that their bodies
might be dishonored among them.
For they exchanged
the truth of God for a lie,
And worshiped and served the
creature
rather than the Creator . . .
For this reason
God gave them over
to degrading passions;
for their women
exchanged the natural function
for that which is unnatural,
And in the same way
also the men
abandoned the natural function
of the woman
and burned in their desire
towards one another,
men with men committing indecent
acts
and receiving in their own persons
the due penalty of their error.
And, although they know
the ordinance of God,
that those who practice such things
are worthy of death,
they not only do the same,
but also give hearty approval
to those who practice them.

(Romans 1:21-27, 32)

The Cult Of Babylon

Satan was victorious over Babylon, and his angels must have gloated over this victory . . . for Babylon means, "Gate of God."

Babylon may not have been the oldest city in Babylonia (about 3000 B.C.), but it became the most important. Babylon was situated in central Mesopotamia on the river Euphrates (in present day Iraq). It is this river that plays an important part at the close of the Tribulation Period in the Battle of Armageddon (Revelation 9:14; 16:12).

It was known as *"Babel"* under Nimrod. You may recall that Nimrod was the son of Cush. Cush was the son of Ham who was the son of Noah. Shortly after the flood, the first Empire was built under Nimrod. The men of Shinar attempted to build a Tower of Babel *"whose top may reach unto heaven"* (Genesis 11:1-9). These towers or *"ziggurats"* were built for worship of pagan deities. And God brought judgment by confounding their language so they could not understand each other.

But the cult of Babylonia grew.

Growth Of Pantheism

The Sumerian culture introduced two groups of gods which brought pantheism into existence. Pantheism is the doctrine that God is not a person, but that all forces are manifestations of God. Pantheism advocates tolerance of the worship of all the gods of various cults.

They worshipped:

Anum	- the sky god and king of the gods
Enlil	- the god of the winds
Enki	- the god of the earth
Utu	- the god of the sun
Innin	- the lady of the heaven, later called Venus
Ishtar	- the god of love and war

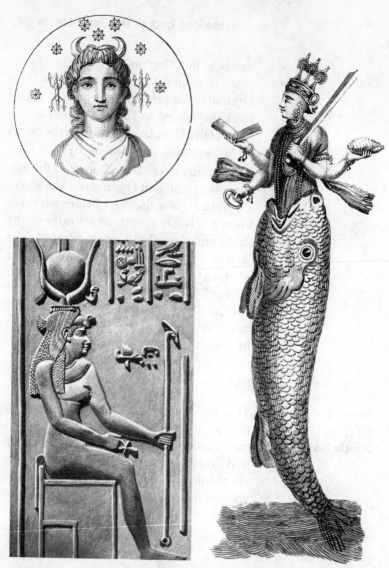

(Top left) Ashtaroth (Ishtar/Babylonian Mother of god). (Bottom left) Isis, goddess of nature in ancient Egypt. (Right) Dagon, Philistine and Phoenician God of agriculture.

Among the witchcraft practices in that day were the interpretation of dreams, astrology, the slaughtering of animals and examining their organs to determine future events. Omens could be obtained even by watching ants.

Worship Of God Of The Sun

Marduk became the high god and patron saint of the city of Babylon, and eventually this god was worshipped beyond the Babylonian Empire.

His name first appears about 2000 B.C. Marduk became the god of the sun. His influence was found in the styles and ceremonial procedures of that day.

The men, as well as women, wore their hair long. Sometimes the men even had dangled curles. The women wore occult amulets.

The King was initiated by priests, swearing allegiance to the god <u>Bel</u>, the god of heaven and earth, and carried the image of Marduk in procession through the streets.

Activity was centered around the temples ... and the wealth of the temples grew. When the army won a battle, the first share of food and slaves went to the temple. The priests were more powerful than the king, for they were the guardians of the gods. It is estimated that by the ninth century before Christ there were some 65,000 different gods.

Every family had household gods.

Bisexual Deity

Ishtar (*Astarte* to the Greeks, *Ashtoreth* to the Jews) was a combined Aphrodite and

Venus, often pictured as a bisexual deity.
The Babylonians offered this prayer to
Ishtar, the Mother of their god:

> I beseech thee, Ishtar,
>   Queen of all cities, leader of all men.
> Thou art the light of the world,
>   thou art the light of heaven . . .
> Supreme is thy might, O lady,
>   exalted art thou above all gods . . .
> At thy name
>   the earth and heavens shake,
>   and the gods they tremble . . .
> Where thou glancest,
>   the dead come to life,
>   and the sick rise and walk;
>   the mind of the diseased is healed
>   when it looks upon thy face . . .

Babylonians had no hope of immortality.
Like the Greeks they believed the dead
went to a dark and shadowy realm within
the bowels of the earth, and none of them
saw the light again. Heaven was only for
the gods.

The priest frequently sacrificed a lamb on
Babylonian altars. To satisfy their god
Marduk, they annointed the idols with oil,
burned incease before them, and offered
up the virginity of their daughters in the
great festival of Ishtar.

**The
Immoral
Act
Imposed
On
Women**

Babylonians had a fear of demons. They
carried magic amulets to ward them off.

Every woman was obliged, once in her life,
to sit in the temple of Venus and submit to
immoral acts before she could return
home. This was to be an offering to the god
of love, Ishtar. At the temple, prostitutes
were in abundance.

The Babylonians and Assyrians practiced various types of magic and fortune telling. There were many practicioners of astrology. The rituals of exorcism was practiced against demons. Priests were engaged in casting spells. A magician's wand was used to draw a circle around those the priest wished to protect. Special chants were repeated over and over again.

While Ishtar was the Babylonian name for the god of love, known as the Queen of Heaven; the Greeks called her Astarte and she is called in the Old Testament, "*Ashtoreth,*" which means in Hebrew, "*shame.*" She was known as the mother of Baal.

You may remember in Judges, chapters 2 and 6, when Gideon pulled down his father's altar of Baal and cut down the Ashtoreth symbol, that he did so by night because he was too afraid to do it by day.

Astarte (Ishtar, Ashtoreth) was associated with the moon, and often shown with the horns of the crescent moon. The temple attendants were eunuchs who wore white robes with pointed caps.

Horns have become the symbol of power. Astarte was adorned on her own head with a bull's head as the ensign of royalty. Horns, crescent moon, pointed caps all are occult symbols which are still used today.

Scene shows worship of Bel, patron god of Babylon. The Lord promised: "I will punish Bel in Babylon, and I will bring forth out of his mouth that which he hath swallowed up; and the nations shall not flow together any more unto him: yea, the wall of Babylon shall fall" (Jeremiah 51:44).

**The
Worship
Of
Mithras**

During the period between 1400 B.C. and 400 A.D. the Persians, Indians, Romans, and Greeks worshiped the god <u>Mithras.</u>

In the age of the Hittites, Mithras is invoked as a god before whom an oath may be sworn. Mithras was a god of friendship and was closely connected with sun worship. The sacrifice of bulls was part of the Mithraic cult.

The Mithras cult was strong among the Roman Praetorian Guards. They worshiped in underground grottos in Rome that would hold about 100 men.

There were seven grades of initiation into the Mithraic mysteries, each with a symbolic name:

corax	(raven)
nymphus	(bridegroom)
miles	(soldier)
leo	(lion)
Perses	(Persian)
heliodromus	(courier to the sun)
pater	(father)

Each initiate was bound and beaten to test his courage. He then submitted to a baptism, and with eyes masked would kneel down to the leader (who wears a pointed cap). At the end of the ceremony he prostrated himself stretched out, humbly on the ground.

SunDay
A Special Day... A Special Relationship.

Sun Basks in Special Day

Songs, Dances Staged To Push Solar Energy

Bulletin Wire Services

The sun, hailed as our cleanest source of energy and already used to supply double the power of the

$350,000 at 6.5 percent interest, and to give government backing to loans of up to $500,000 made by banks at interest up to 10 percent.

7

WORSHIP OF THE SUN BEGAN IN EGYPT

**Sun
Day
Reflects
Sun
Cult**

On Wednesday, May 3, 1978, the United States paid homage to the sun. It was called Sun Day. President Carter flew to Colorado to deliver a speech to the Solar Energy Research Institute. There were sunrise services and solar displays by both industry and the U.S. army. About 12,000 people attended the speechmaking at the Washington monument. The entire United States population had its attention focused on the SUN.

Why? Because national leaders believe the sun offers man's last hope of survival in a day of depleting energy. The sun is man's last hope for life . . . on this earth! Many turned to the sun in awed worship.

The worship of the sun is not new. Over 3000 years ago the Egyptians worshipped the sun. While the Babylonians called the sun, Utu, the Egyptians called it, Ra (or Re). The center of worship was at Heliopolis.

Pharaohs were known as the *"Son of the Sun."* Sun worship in Egypt gradually spread to the solar cult of Rome. In the 3rd century A.D., the Emperor Heliogabalus created the cult called, Sol Invictus; the *"Unconquered Sun."* And in 274 A.D. the Emperor Aurelian built a large temple in Rome to Sol Invictus.

Sun And Eroticism

Sun worship is the real religion of India even today. Hindus have several distinct sects of sun worshipers. At Konarak, India a spectacular sun temple has been built linking the sun cult and the fertility cult. The temple is adorned with erotic sculptures.

The sun plays a dominating role in astrology and the interpreting of horoscopes.

Some claim that Masonry came to Northern Africa and Asia Minor from the lost continent of Atlantis, originating as Sun and Fire worship. Thus we can see why most Christians will not be associated with Masons nor any other secret organization.

Not only did the Egyptians worship the sun, they also worshiped the moon, the bull, the crocodile, the hawk, the cow, the baboon, the goat, and many other animals. The goat and bull were especially sacred to the Egyptians as representing sexual creative powers.

The priests were kept busy selling their charm amulets, mumbling incantations, performing magical rites promising eternal life to those who would purchase their "prayed over" charms.

**Moses
Warns
Israel**

Moses, realizing the danger of sun worship, revealed God's warning:

> . . . beware,
> lest you lift up your eyes to heaven
> and see the sun
> and the moon and the stars,
> all the host of heaven,
> and be drawn away
> and worship them and serve them . . .
>
> (Deuteronomy 4:19)

When Josiah became king of Judah in 642 B.C., there was gross idolatry in the land — Baal altars, star and planet worship, the sacrifice of children to the god Moloch, astrology, occultism, worship of the sun.

Some of the gods Egyptians worshipped besides the sun and moon.

Josiah ordered that all this be destroyed and abolished:

> The king commanded the priests to
>   bring out of the temple of the Lord
>   all the vessels
>   that were made for Baal . . .
>   and he burned them outside Jerusalem.
>
> And he did away
>   with the idolatrous priests . . .
>   who burned incense to Baal,
>   to the sun and to the moon
>   and to the constellations
>   and to all the host of heaven.
>
> And he brought out the Asherah
>   (goddess of love)
>   from the house of the Lord . . .
>   and burned it in the brook Kidron . . .
>
> He also broke down the houses
>   of the male cult prostitutes
>   which were in the house of the
>   Lord . . .
>
> And he did away with the horses
>   which the kings of Judah
>   had given to the sun . . .
>   and he burned the chariots of the sun
>   with fire.
>
> And all the priests of the high places
>   who were there
>   he slaughtered on the altars;
>   and burned human bones on them;
>   then he returned to Jerusalem.
>   (2 Kings 23:4-7, 11, 20)

Such was the judgment exercised against the gross idolatry of that day. But we have come full circle for today we again are beginning to worship the sun, pagan idols, the cult of Baal and its gross immorality, the occult, and signs in the heavens.

8

THE RISE OF THE DRUIDS

**Rise
Of
Secret
Societies**

Druids are mentioned by name in some 30 references by Greek and Roman writers between the 2nd century B.C. and the 4th century A.D.

Druids are a member of a Celtic religious order of mystic priests who originated in ancient Britain, Ireland, and France.

The word Druid means *"the men of the oak trees."*

About 1245 A.D. a gathering of Druids was held with representatives from many geographical regions and the objectives of the Order of Druids was agreed upon. A grove was founded in England which still exists today, Mount Hawmus Grove.

Druids, along with Rosicrucians and Freemasons are a mixture of mystical-occult societies which were influenced by the mystic Jacob Boehme.

Jacob Boehme propounded the theory that the Trinity was: (1) the sky, (2) the sun, and (3) the light. Boehme further believed that just as God is threefold, so man, being created in the image of God, is threefold. This is how Boehme developed the THRICE BORN or THREE BIRTHS theology. It should be noted that several very prominent "Christians" claim to be "thrice born." The origin of such statements can only be attributed to witchcraft and the occult.

Boehme reasoned:

1. The "elemental birth" gives man his body.
2. The "astral birth" gives him his instincts and intelligence, which he shares with the other animals.
3. The "spiritual birth" gives man the "divine essence," the ingredient in him which is potentially God.

Boehme combined Christian mysticism and Cabbala, an occult numerical philosophy developed by Jewish Rabbis in the Middle Ages.

Council Of 13

The Druids picked up some of this philosophy and incorporated it into their mysticism. The secret teachings of the Druids were never written, but were communicated orally to specially prepared candidates. Such practices continue today in modern day witchcraft in the Council of 13, and in the Mason's Council of 33.

The Imitation Of Christianity

The Druids, as do witches of today, believed in reincarnation. They believed in a purgatorial type of hell where they would be purged of their sins, afterward passing on to the happiness of unity with the gods. The Druids taught that all men would be saved, but that some must return to earth many times to learn the lessons of human life and to overcome the inherent evil of their own nature.

Before a candidate was entrusted with the secret doctrines of the Druids, he was bound with a vow of secrecy. These doctrines were revealed only in the depths of forests and in the darkness of caves.

The Druids celebrated a number of feast days. At dawn on the 25th day of December, the birth of the Sun God was cele-

THE ARCH-DRUID IN HIS CEREMONIAL ROBES.

KIS meant "Holy the God of the Septenary." "Septenary" means seven.

Witches in California performing an act of worship at dusk.

brated. The Druids had a Madonna, or Virgin Mother, with a Child in her arms; and their Sun God was resurrected at the time of the year corresponding to that at which we celebrate Easter. It is amazing how Satan becomes the great imitator.

The Druids worshiped the sun, moon and stars. They also worshiped the serpent. The famous Stonehenge in Southwestern England is a Druid altar.

Initiates had to pass through three degrees of the Druidic Mysteries. Few successfully passed them all. They included burying the candidate in a coffin . . . sending him out to sea in an open boat. Those who reached the third degree became prominent British religious and political leaders.

Druids came out of the Celtic culture. The Celts practiced human sacrifice. They sacrificed adults as well as infants and had ritual drownings. The number three was sacred to the Celts. Such mysticism and occultism became part of the Druid tradition.

Druid priests exist today . . . and evidence indicates that ritual sacrifice is also still in some areas practiced today.

The controversial John Todd, one who claims conversion out of witchcraft, says that prior to 1972 he was a Grand Druid High Priest of the Council of 13. He has also claimed that the conspiracy of Druidism witchcraft is undermining the world and even infiltrating into the Christian church, Sunday schools and the Christian school system.

9

A SECRET FROM ANCIENT ISRAEL

**Cabala
An Occult
Society**

While the Prophets of Israel gave us our entire Old Testament and almost all of our New Testament, a few out of this nation also gave us the Cabala writings. Cabala is an occult society which was developed by certain Jewish rabbis. The oldest Cabalistic book was probably penned in 120 AD by Rabbi Akiba. It was based on a mystical interpretation of the Scriptures. It was popularized in southern France and Spain in the 12th and 13th centuries.

Cabala is sometimes spelled Cabbala or Qabbalah. The Hebrew word is Kabbalah. This means "*receiving*" or "*that which is received.*" The word Kabbalah implied the handing down of tradition. Many believe that this secret lore began with the Essenes.

The Essenes flourished from about 2 BC to 135 AD. They were mostly unmarried and filled their ranks by newcomers joining them and by their adopting other people's children. They were required to take secret oaths. They had their own purification rites. Many of them perished in the Roman wars.

The name Essenes supposedly is derived from an ancient Syrian word meaning *"physician."* Membership in this order was only possible after a year of probation. This secret sect had three degrees of progression that members had to go through.

The Essenes, like the Gnostics, were emanationists (the drawing out of something from a source). One of their chief aims was the reinterpretation of the Mosaic law according to certain secret spiritual keys. Some have even attempted to show that Jesus was reared and educated by the Essenes and later initiated into this mystic order. There is no evidence for such a "guess."

Mystic Links

This mystic *"christianity"* continues today with books that state that Jesus and Bacchus were interrelated. One book seeks to allege that the surname of Joseph's family was Panther. They develop this theme from what they state are some early Jewish commentaries which say that a man was healed "in the name of Jesus ben Panther." It was Bacchus who was nursed by panthers (in Greek and Roman mythology). The skin of the panther was also sacred in some Egyptian initiatory ceremonials.

These cult books try also to link the monogram abbreviation IHS (the first, second and last letters of the Greek name Jesus . . . IHSUS) with Bacchus. They state that IHS in the Greek has a numerical value of

608 . . . which is the secret number of Bacchus.

From the background of mysticism, Cabala had its origins. They were reminiscent of the Gnostics who flourished in the 2nd Century AD. The Gnostics believed that people could be saved through a secret knowledge[1].

The Zohar

The principal source of the Cabala is the Zohar. The Zohar is a mystical commentary on the Pentateuch, the first five books of the Old Testament, written from the 2nd to the 13th century. The Cabala theology was not only Israel and the entire cosmos in need of salvation but even God Himself. For, they believe, that every stone, every plant shelters a divine spark which yearns to return to its origin . . . cries out for salvation!

The term *"Cabala"* soon penetrated the European languages and by the 17th century it was closely associated with magic. In the 19th and 20th century it has grown to include diverse kinds of occult practice and divination (fortune telling).

---

[1] Gnostics believed that salvation depended solely upon the knowledge of one's *"spiritual"* nature. This gave them license to live a life of sin. In fact, some Gnostic leaders urged their followers to sin. They taught that promiscuity was God's law and that since they were *"pearls,"* they could not be stained by any external mud. Many believed that humans were originally unisex . . . that the creation of woman was the source of evil. They taught that Jesus was merely a man. They also believed in hundreds of divine powers emanating or coming out of God.

The 22 major cards of the Tarot pack are connected with the 22 Paths used by those who practiced Cabala. Tarot cards are "*fortune telling*" cards.

The three major books of Cabala are the Sepher Yetzirah (The Book of Formation), Sepher ha Zohar (The Book of Splendor) and the Apocalypse (The Book of Revelation). These were probably written about 120 AD.

Magic Symbols

The Cabala taught that there existed within God's Word a hidden doctrine which was the key to Scriptures. This is symbolized by the crossed keys upon the papal crest. Cult books themselves point out that the theories of Cabalism are interwoven with the doctrines of magic, of Rosicrucianism and Freemasonry.

The Tetragrammaton (meaning 4 letters) were the four consonants of the ancient Hebrew name for God. Generally spelled JHVH or YHWH, the name of God was considered too sacred to be spoken in utterance.

The Cabalists used the Tetragrammaton as a sort of magic talisman. The use of it in this manner found its way into European magic as one of the major "*names of power.*"

John Reuchlin (a "Christian" Cabalist of the 16th century) maintained that the name of Jesus (the Pentagrammaton) exceeds the Tetragrammaton in power by adding the letter S to it. Thus JHVH becomes JHSVH.

Cabalists had a preoccupation with letters and names of God, as containers of secret knowledge. Circular symbol at left, hung around the neck before sunrise on a Sunday was supposed to make the wearer invisible. Triangular symbol at right shows the Hebrew letter W, used to signify the trinity sapphires *(Sephiroth)*.

 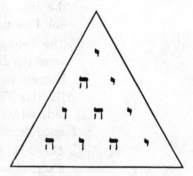

Diagram square at left was supposed to give the magician control of all evil spirits. The Tetragrammaton (meaning 4 letters) were the four consonants of the ancient Hebrew name for God. By arranging the four letters of the *"Great Name of God,"* Cabalists believed the 72 powers of the *"Great Name of God"* were manifested.

Since names of power were believed to work automatically, cultists used these names to attempt to further their ulterior motives.

5-Pointed Star

The Cabalist and cultists carried the 5 letter symbol further. Penta means 5 thus Penta-grammaton (the five letters for Jesus . . . JHSVH). The star with its 5 points became to the cultists a weapon of power in magic.

A pentagram (5-pointed star) with one of its points projecting upwards was to them a symbol of the divine spirit. A reversed pentagram (with 2 points projecting upwards, represents a symbol of evil and suggest the horns of the Devil.

Modern magicians use the pentagram. In gnostic schools, the pentagram is called the blazing star and denotes the sign of intellectual omnipotence. The Order of the Golden Dawn (formed by 3 members of the Rosicrucian Society in England) has two rituals using the Pentagram:

The Lesser Ritual of the Pentagram
The Supreme Invoking Ritual of the
    Pentagram

In Golden Dawn ritual the pentagram was used *"if there may arise an absolute necessity for working or conversing with a Spirit of an evil nature."*

Ritual Continues Today

The Cabala philosophies are shunned by most Jews today. However, with the recent mushrooming of witchcraft and secret societies, many of the doctrines of the Cabala are again being expounded. Many of today's secret societies borrow on ideas first propagated by those who departed from the Scriptures about 2000 years ago.

God had long ago reminded the people of Israel that if they would follow Him as David did that blessing would come. God also warned them that if they did not follow Him

and forsake my statues . . .
and shall go and serve other gods,
and worship them;
Then will I pluck them up by the roots
out of my land
which I have given them . . .
                    (2 Chronicles 7:19,20)

Those that saw this occurring to Israel would ask why the Lord scattered this nation and allowed them to suffer hardships. God's answer was:

Because they forsook
the Lord God of their fathers,
which brought them out of the land of
Egypt, and laid hold on other gods,
and worshipped them, and served them:
therefore
hath He brought all this evil upon them.
                    (2 Chronicles 7:22)

This is not to imply that all the evil cults of today had their origin from Hebrews of yesterday. This is simply not true! While many of the people of Israel did reject God many times throughout the pages of Scripture and worship evil gods . . . the Gentiles were even more guilty in their pursuit of evil!

ZIONISM
by
Gary G. Cohen

In antiquity, the southwest upper hill of Jerusalem was called, Zion. Later, still in the Old Testament Davidic period, the entire city of Jerusalem became known as Zion. Eventually, the entire land of Palestine came to be called Zion.

Zionism is thus the movement to establish a national home-land for the Jewish people in their ancient biblical land. The national anthem of the State of Israel reflects this—its title being, *Ha Tikvah,* "The Hope." The words were written in 1878 by Nephtali Imber, a Hebrew poet, and the music by Samuel Cohen, a pioneer settler in Rishon Le Zion ("First to Zion"), Palestine. Its words go, in a haunting resolute Hebrew melody, as follows:

The eye toward Zion constantly is turned,
Then *our hope* it is not dead,
The ancient longing will be fulfilled,
To return to the land—the land of our fathers,
The city of Jerusalem, Where David encamped.

Only those who have studied the *century after century perse-cutions* against the Jews—in Russia, in England, in Germany, out of France, out of Africa, out of Spain, and then the Holo-caust under Hitler—can begin to appreciate and to feel the desperation of the Jews for the end of the endless attacks upon them and their children.

It was within such an atmosphere that a 36 year old Austrian lawyer, Theodore Herzl, a Jew, witnessed in 1896 the Dreyfus Affair—the degradation of a French Jewish military captain as a spy. By 1906 Dreyfus was proven innocent. The antisemitism which once again caught part of Europe convinced Herzl that the only true solution for Jewish freedom was for Jews to migrate back to Palestine—"Israel"—which at that time had already been held for centuries by the Turks and still belonged to them.

Herzl on February 14, 1896, in Vienna, published his monumental pamphlet of about 90 pages entitled, *Der Judenstaat* (The Jewish State). In it his central theme is to call upon the Jews of the world to unite because of their common misery, and to recognize that the only solution is to return to their biblical homeland. While some laughed, Herzl prophecied that within fifty years he would be known as the Father of the State of Israel.

August 29–31, 1897 saw the First Zionist Congress assemble in Basle, Switzerland, and congresses met annually afterward. This began the efforts . . . contacting the Rothschilds for help . . . meeting the Kaiser of Germany in Palestine . . . meeting Sultans . . . expeditions to buy land and reversals . . . which finally resulted in 1917, at the close of World War I, in the British League of Nations Mandate over Palestine . . . and then on May 14, 1948 in the establishment of the State of Israel.

Herzl died at 44, was buried in Vienna, and as his will requested, was moved to Israel after it took Jerusalem. He now is buried on Mt. Herzl, Jerusalem, under a huge black granite monument which has no writing upon it, except for four Hebrew letters, HRZL. He is now recognized, as was his youthful prediction, as the Father of the State of Israel.

In the early 1900's some naive Jewish Zionists, knowing of the anti-Jewish persecutions by the Russian Tzars, publically lauded and marched in favor of the Bolshevik communist take-over in Russia. It was perhaps this, along with the usual anti-Jewish feelings, that caused some to jump upon this and to label communism a Jewish plot and to equate Zionism with revolution. The Jewish people themselves soon discovered, as Israel knows too well today, that the anti-God and anti-Christian communists were also anti-Jewish, anti-Israel, and anti-Zionist. Equating Zionism as the force behind communism must be seen as absolutely false, and if anything, another part of Satan's strategy to destroy Israel before God fully fills His promises pronounced in Romans 11:26, and in other places, to someday convert Israel to Christ, Zechariah 12:10.

Sin is the cause of the world's woes, and the Middle East has always seethed with turmoil, amid the Arabs, British, French, Germans, etc., even before Hitler forced the European Jews out of Europe and into Israel. *Zionism* is the movement to establish a national homeland for the Jewish people in Palestine. Read Ezekiel 36, 37, 38 on this, as well as Zechariah chapters 12–14. God clearly will eventually give them the land.

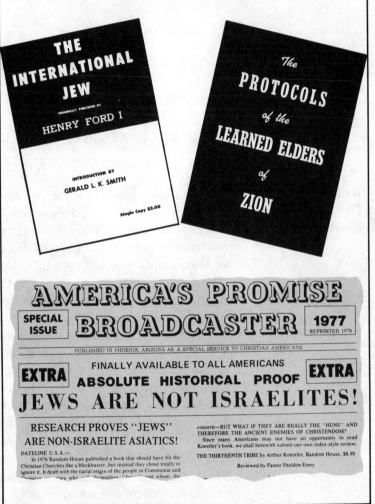

Some of the anti-Jewish literature.

10

CHINA ... CULTS OF CONFUSION

**Dynasty
Of
Death**

Reliable Chinese history does not go back any further than 776 BC. Some Chinese attempt to describe the creation of the world as occurring in 2,229,000 BC. They state that P' an Ku was the first man . . . that he labored for 18,000 years hammering the universe into shape for its ultimate creation.

In 2852 BC began a succession of five rulers who governed the Empire with a cruel hand and were considered atheists. This dynasty was brought to an end by the wicked Emperor Chieh. He amused himself and his wife by compelling 3000 Chinese to jump to death in a lake of wine! China gave birth to humanistic philosophies. Humanism is an atheistic philosophy which holds that man is capable of self-fulfillment without recourse to God.

I-Ching

It was China that spawned that humanistic, metaphysical book called *I-Ching*, or *"Book of Changes."* Their theory was that there was a single cosmic cell containing *"ether" (Ch'i)* which was made to pulsate by a creative force known as *Tao*.

Tension set up by this activity eventually split the cell into opposite and complementary halves. Thus twin ethers which encompassed the universe were called by them, *Yin* and *Yang*.

Yin / is of the earth, dark, female.
Yang / is of heaven, bright, male.

The Chinese believe that the continuous operation of Tao (which they suppose to be a natural law), causes Yin and Yang to alternate and by this process five *"elements"* are produced: water, fire, wood, metal and earth. Thus evolves the creation process.

The Chinese used *I-Ching* (*The Book of Changes*) as a manual for telling the future.

Yin and Yang

In Chinese philosophy, two great opposite principles or forces, on whose interplay everything in the universe depends; Yang is male, light and positive, Yin is female, dark and negative, and all phenomena can be classified in terms of them; in Taoism, the Tao is the principle which unites and transcends the opposites.

Confucius edited the volume adding commentary. He ranked it above all other writings and wished that he might be free to spend 50 years in its study.

China encompasses three basic religions: Confucianism, Buddhism and Taoism. Lao Tze, born in 604 BC, is the traditional founder of Taoism. The beliefs of Taoism are found in the book, *Tao Te Ching*. Taoists claim that it enshrines the wisdom of the universe. The Taoist *"bible"* mushroomed from one small book to over 5000 volumes! Tao means *"course or way."* Its teachings are paradoxical, irrational, confusing. Taoism points to no particular way. Taoism has evolved into an elaborate hierarchy of priest-magicians, both male and female . . . specialists in various branches of Chinese occultism. They combine the role of medium, oracle, sorcerer and physician.

Taoists And Acupuncture

Credited to Taoist origins are astrology and acupuncture. Acupuncture is a system of healing where needles are inserted into the skin to a depth of about a tenth of an inch. They are left in for a few minutes and then removed. The impression of magic comes from the fact that the needles are often inserted into points which have no apparent connection with the ailment that is being treated. Acupuncturists usually attack hay fever by treating the liver. A needle stuck into the little toe is said to cure a headache. Acupuncture is based on the Yin and Yang philosophy. The Chinese attitude to medicine is that attention must be given to keep the individual healthy . . . not wait for him to get sick and then treat him. Chinese patients paid the doctor as long as they stayed healthy and stopped paying him when they fell ill!

When the Yin and Yang energies in a man's body are reasonably in balance, he is healthy. If one becomes too strong or too weak, he is ill.

Taoists And Astrology

While Taoists are credited with starting astrology, it first began in Babylon. Astrology is the pseudo-science which claims to foretell the future by studying the supposed influence of the relative positions of the moon, sun and stars on human affairs. Astronomy, however, is an exact science which studies the stars, planets and all other heavenly bodies, dealing with their composition, motion, relative position and size.

The Taoists incorporated all the floating traditions of Chinese magic and sorcery (witchcraft). They gave rise to a number of secret societies, many of which became bandits and ruled large parts of China for more than 18 centuries.

Confucius An Agnostic

Confucius (Kung Fu-tze/550-480 BC) developed his own cult which was practiced in Chinese temples. Much of the traditional Chinese view of the universe, the gods and human morality and conduct is based on his teachings.

Confucius taught that heaven was approachable for knowledge of the future only by the Emperor, and it was from heaven that he obtained his mandate to rule on earth. Confucianism did not uphold belief in the survival of the soul. Confucius was an agnostic. Man had no special destiny and Confucius did not believe in eternal life.

It is a strange coincidence of history that the 6th century BC saw the birth of 4 world religions. For Israel, that century marked the soul-shaking experience of the Babylonian captivity (606-536 BC) and the subsequent restoration of the nation's life with the rebuilding of the Temple (520-16 BC). This began a fresh start to the already active system we know as Judaism.

At that same period, Confucianism began. In 567 BC, in northern India, Buddha was born. While at the same time in Iran, Zoroaster was preaching a religion that would also influence millions.

Many Gods

The Chinese believed in many gods. There were city gods who were supposed to guard cities. There were kitchen gods. There was a goddess of the bedroom. She was in charge of married couples and their children and usually "shared a bed." Even bandits had their gods.

Some gods did double duty. The kitchen god was also the patron god of professional cooks. The officials were to worship these gods, but they also reserved the right to punish them for failing to perform their duties (such as bring rain or cure an epidemic). A confusion of cults clouded

Chinese religious thinking including such secret societies as the Triad Society.

Out of this background emerged atheistic communism. In 1945 the Chinese communists launched a civil war driving Chiang-Kai-shek's forces to Taiwan. The People's Republic of China was proclaimed October 1, 1949. In recent years relations between China and the United States have thawed. Meanwhile, however, the bamboo curtain has successfully kept out any major evangelical thrust into China. Show window churches for tourists are allowed to exist, but Christianity is still subtly but firmly suppressed throughout China.

Nevertheless, the seed of the Gospel sown in China by such missionary giants as Hudson Taylor, Jonathan Goforth, C.T. Studd, F.C. Dreyer and others in the early 1900's is still bearing bits of precious fruit today!

Chinese children are now taught atheistic principles.

11

THE STRANGE BELIEFS IN INDIA

**India
And
Animism**

India is a nation of nearly two million square miles. It is 20 times the size of Great Britain and has more people than in all North and South America combined! Within its borders live one-fifth of the population of the earth.

The oldest known religion in India was *Animism* ... the worship of stones, animals, trees, streams, mountains and stars. Snakes were considered divine symbols of virile reproductive power. Some spirits were considered good; others, evil. They believed that only great skill in magic could keep the body from being possessed or tortured. This strange theology is contained in their book *Atharva-Veda* or *Book of the Knowledge of Magic.*

The most important Vedic god was Agni-fire. He was the sacred flame that lifted the sacrifice to heaven. The most popular figure was Indra, wielder of thunder and storm.

Indra's favorite enemy was Krishna, who in the *Vedas* was as yet only the local god of the Krishna tribe.

The creation of the earth is described as God falling into two pieces. From these pieces arose a man and a woman. Then in a series of human reproduction acts came cows, bulls, other cattle, etc. down to ants. This is described in *Brihadaranyaka Upanishad*, i,4; Hume 81.

Sacrifice Of The Horse

Ritualistic altars were set up. The strangest ritual of all was the *Ashvamedha*, or Sacrifice of the Horse ... an obscene ritual which involved the queen of the tribe. This occurred in the period about 1000-500 BC.

Upanishads were a group of philosophers who made a study of the universe. *Upa* means, near and *shad*, to sit. The idea was that those who sat nearest the teacher came to know the deepest secrets of the universe.

In a 300 year period there evolved some 108 discourses on philosophy and religion. They sought to answer in these discourses the questions: "*Whence are we born, where do we live, and whither do we go?*"

The Three Steps

From this religion strange rites were born in this secret doctrine. The **first** step was called *Atman*. It proposed that the essence of our own self is not the body, or the mind, or the individual ego, but the silent and formless depth of being within us.

The **second** step is Brahman. Brahman, is this sense, means the impersonal Soul of the World. This is not to be confused with the word, Brahma who is a member of the Hindu triad of gods (Brahma, Vishnu, Shiva).

The Atman is the Soul of all Souls. The Brahman is the Soul of all Things.

The **third** step is considered the most important of all. It is that Atman and Brahman are one. Confusing? All cults thrive on confusion and mysticism!

The Upanishads (teachers) burn this doctrine into the minds of their pupils with untiring repetition.

The Jains

About the middle of the 6th century BC, a boy was born to a wealthy nobleman in the province of Bihar. His parents belonged to a sect that looked upon rebirth as a curse, upon suicide as a privilege. When their son reached age 31, the parents ended their lives by voluntary starvation. The young man spent 13 years in self-denial, walking through the streets without any clothing . . . seeking self-purification.

He was hailed by a group of disciples as a Jina (conqueror). They called him Mahavira or the Great Hero. This sect gradually developed into a sect called Jains. They regarded Mahavira as the last of a long line of saviours . . . the 24th saviour. Mahavira lived during the same time as Buddha but there is no indication they ever met, though they espoused their religions in the same country.

The Jains sect split into two factions:

The Digambaras (space-clad or naked)
The Svetambaras (white-clad)

The Jain philosophy is very pessimistic and evolves around 6 basic spheres of belief. Today, both sects wear clothes. There are only about 1.5 million Jains in India. Comparatively speaking it is considered a very small sect. Gandhi was strongly influenced by the Jains. Eventually he may be named their 25th saviour.

The Buddha

About the year 567 BC, in northern India, Gotama was born. He became known as the *Buddha* (the enlightened one). He founded a religion that was destined to spread throughout a large part of Asia.

Buddhists believe in many demons and spirits. Buddhism denies that there is a personal world-creator. It denies that there is an immortal soul. It believes that there is a personal continuity from life to life through many rebirths (reincarnation).

Buddha passed from agnosticim to outright atheism. He did not forbid the popular worship of gods. He frowned at the idea that one could pray to the *"Unknowable."* He did not believe in either a heaven or hell.

Aims Of Buddhism

Buddhism's basic aim is to achieve enlightenment. To achieve this enlightenment one must get off of the endless wheel of birth, death, rebirth, and again, birth,

Buddhists believe in many demons and spirits.

death, rebirth, etc. Getting away from this cycle was called reaching Nirvana.

Nirvana was described as the state of perfect blessedness achieved by the extinction of individual existence.

To reach Nirvana, one is told he must follow the Holy Eightfold Path: 1. right views, 2. right intention, 3. right speech, 4. right action, 5. right livelihood, 6. right effort 7. right mindfulness and 8. right concentration.

He taught what he called Four Holy Truths:

1. Life is full of suffering.
2. The source of suffering is craving for sensual pleasure, for afterlife, and for annihilation.
3. There is an end of suffering when craving ceases.
4. There is a path which leads to this ending, the Holy Eightfold Path.

They have another formula for the Path called the "three trainings" of 1. morality, 2. concentration and 3. wisdom.

Under morality, they observe 5 basic precepts. Particular importance is placed on not harming human or animal life.

Under concentration, one contemplates his body, the feelings, mental states and dharmas (doctrines). You watch your breath go in and out. You become aware of each action ... walking, sitting, lying down, etc.

Under wisdom, three grades are distinguished. The lowest grade is based on hearing the doctrine, the next on thinking about what has been heard . . . the highest on meditative trances.

Such fruits of meditation are supposed to give to one magic powers (walking on water, body projection into space, the ability to hear sounds not actually present).

Rise Of Hinduism

Buddha died in 483 BC at the age of 80.

Hinduism assimilated much of the Buddhist cult religion. Hinduism has no founder. "Hindu" is a Persian word that simply means "*Indian.*" Hinduism espouses many gods. Its literature which reveals its confusing theology is called the Veda.

The Hindus have an array of personal gods. Among them is the god Rudra who is now also known as Shiva. He is also known as Krishna. The supreme god is known as Vishnu.

The Krishna of popular religion today is not the Krishna of original Hinduism, but a Krishna who was developed about the 9th century AD.

Tantrists And Magic

Shiva represents an austere deity and Shakti, the female counterpart. From this emerged one of the most satanic cults of the East, Tantrism. Much of the Western cult practices have been influenced by the Tantrists of India. From them has come the ceremonial magic of candles, incense, bells, magical wands, spells, magic circles, bodily postures, occult gestures, symbolical designs and words of "power."

Tantrism includes the exposure of the body to the sun, the attempt to control body functions that are automatic in nature (body temperature, pulse rates, reflexes, etc.). Yoga is said to have its origins in this strange cult. Tantrism is shunned by Hinduists and Buddhists because it dwells on sexual excessiveness, advocating complete sexual freedom ... which is worshipped as a god.

From early days Hindu society was divided into four castes or social units. It is based on the idea that men are born with different spiritual qualities ... which result from their actions in previous existences (reincarnation). The four castes are:

1. Brahmins (priests)
2. Kshatriyas (warriors)
3. Vaisyas (merchants)
4. Sudras (menial laborers, servants)

Mahatma Gandhi combined ideas from many religions believing that all religions were true. In the past few years much of India's multi-religion cults have infiltrated to the West. It has become fashionable, particularly among college students and the educated to seek salvation through the mystics of India. This trend was begun by the Beatles (an English singing group of the 60's) that made a pilgrimage to sit under the teachings of Maharishi Mahesh Yoga.

Yoga
A
Cult

Yoga, which is even taught in many schools in the United States, evolved from these curious cults of India. It is a form of humanism which says: "I am the master of my ship." Its advocates have prescribed it for anything from getting rid of migraine headaches to getting rich. There are many yoga positions ... the most popular one being the cross-legged "_Lotus_" position. Another is standing on your head, controlling your breathing and reciting repetitious phrases (_mantras_).

Standing on your head makes about as much sense as the other forms of Indian mysticism. The only advantage of standing on your head is that you can see the world ... upside down!

12

ISLAM . . . A FORM OF GODLINESS

Birth Of Islam

Mohammed was born in Mecca about 570 AD into a poor family in a country that was three quarters desert. Mecca derived profit both as a religious and commerce center for caravans travelling annually to South Arabia.

Little did the world know at that time that within 100 years these nomads would conquer half of Asia, all Persia (now Iran) and Egypt and most of North Africa!

Living on the desert these people were called Arabs. *Arab* means arid. Almost all the population at that time were nomad Bedouins. They loved horses but the camel was their greatest friend. It travelled at 8 miles an hour, but it could go without water five days in the summer; 25 days in the winter. The camel provided milk, its dung was burned for fuel and when it died, it was eaten by the Bedouins. Its hair and hide made clothing and tents.

The Oppressed Lot Of Women

The women of the Bedouin tribes though of incomparable beauty were considered mere personal property (chattel). They spent a lifetime of drudgery. When a girl was born into a family, the father could

ISLAM

Followers: approx. 800 000 000

Countries:

Afghanistan
Algeria
Bahrain
Bangladesh
Benin
Egypt
Federation of Arabian Emirates (Abu
   Dhabi, Dubai, Ajman, Sharjah, Ras el
   Khaimah, Fujairah, Umm al Qaiwain
Indonesia
Iraq
Iran
Jordan
Qatar
Kuwait
Libya

Morocco
Mauritania
Niger
Oman
Pakistan
Saudi Arabia
Senegal
Somalia
Sudan
Syria
Tunisia
Turkey
Yemen (Arab Republic) = Arab-
   Islamic Republic
Yemen (People's Republic)
   = South Yemen

Moslems saying their prayers as prescribed by the Koran.

bury her at birth, if he so willed. He would mourn her coming and hide his face from his friends. At about age 7 she was sold off to any youth of the clan for marriage . . . at a price! Her husband demanded of her many children. He often had many wives and he could dismiss her at any time. This was the climate in which Mohammad (sometimes spelled Muhammed) was born. His new religion only slightly improved the lot of women. Muhammed himself had 10 wives; other Muslems were permitted 4.

The Arab of that day worshipped many gods of the sky . . . stars and the moon and even what they believed were sacred stones.

Mecca Center Of Worship

The center of this stone reverence was in Mecca. A square structure of stone in Mecca became their holiest shrine in the world. It was called *Kaaba,* which means *cube.* It has been rebuilt about 10 times. They believed the first Kaaba was erected by angels from heaven; the second by Adam; the third by his son Seth; the fourth by Abraham and his son Ishmael by Hagar. The eighth was built in Mohammed's lifetime in 605 AD. The tenth is the square structure now visible today in Mecca.

It was into this climate that Mohammed entered the scene. When he was about 25, a prosperous Meccan widow employed him as her agent in a caravan to Syria. She was so pleased with his success that she (Khadija) married Mohammed. With added leisure he was now able to visit a cave on Mount Hira near Mecca, for meditation.

It must be pointed out that in this era the Kaaba contained several statues representing gods. One was called <u>Allah</u> (the "up" one), a tribal god. Along with Allah were three other gods called Allah's daughters. The Quraish tribe began worshipping Allah as the chief god. He was presented to the Meccans as the Lord of their soil.

Mohammed was illiterate as a young man. He could not read nor write. Mohammed became good friends with his cousin, Waraqah ibn Nawfal, who was well acquainted with the Scriptures of the Hebrews and Christians. In fact, during Mohammed's lifetime, there were many Christians in Arabia. Mohammed frequently visited Medina, where his father had died, and there met many Jews.

Mohammed Starts New Religion

As Mohammed approached 40 he became more absorbed in religion. He was dismayed at the many gods of the Arabs, their constant tribal warfare, their loose morality and their political disunity. These factors influenced him in starting a new religion that had only one god.

Often during the holy month of Ramadan, he would go with his family to a cave three miles from Mecca. Ramadan is the ninth month of the Moslem year. It is a time of daily fasting from sunrise to sunset. One night in the year 610 AD tradition claims that the angel Gabriel appeared to him and commanded him to read. When he awoke, he heard a voice saying: "O Mohammed! thou art the messenger of Allah, and I am Gabriel."

Thereafter he had many such visions. Those near him at the time said they neither saw nor heard any angel. In the next four years Mohammed openly announced himself as the prophet of Allah. His first convert was his aging wife (who was 15 years his senior); his second, his cousin; his third, his servant; his fourth, his kinsman Abu Bekr.

Mohammed Conquers Mecca

Abu Bekr was a man of respected standing among his tribe, the Quraish. He converted five other Meccan leaders. These became the Prophet's six "Companions." Much friction developed among the tribesmen when Mohammed claimed to be a messenger from God. After bitter wars Mohammed conquered Mecca in 630 AD. He cleared away all the idols except the Black Stone in the Kaaba, which is considered holy to this day by Moslems. From then on, to this day, pilgrims must walk around the Kaaba seven times and kiss or salute the Black Stone. The Black Stone, apparently a meteorite, was considered sacred and was built into the wall of the Kaaba.

In the first days, the Muslims adopted several of the Jewish rites. They prayed facing Jerusalem. Jewish fast days were observed. But when relations with the Jews became tense, Muslims were told to face Mecca when they prayed. An annual pilgrimage to Mecca was also ordered. This was done because the Jews (correctly so) disputed his prophetic claims and questioned the accuracy of his so-called vision.

Mohammed Claimed To Be God's Mouthpiece

Mohammed could brook no opposition. He considered himself God's mouthpiece. Asma, a local woman poetess, attacked Mohammed in her rhymes. It cost Asma her life. A Moslem plunged his sword so fervently into the sleeping woman's breast that it affixed her to the couch. Two other poets were also executed. Meanwhile local Jews accused Mohammed of idolatry.

In one battle captured Jews were given the choice of choosing Islam or death. The 600 fighting men chose death. They were slain and buried in the market place of Medina. Their women and children were sold into slavery.

This climate of "justice" has pervaded down through the centuries and is one of the reasons for tension in the Middle East. In 630 AD Mohammed proclaimed Mecca the Holy City of Islam. He decreed that no unbeliever should ever be allowed to set foot on its sacred soil.

Mohammed's Barren Wives

Mohammed had 10 wives and 2 concubines. All of his wives, except his first, Khadija, were barren. Mohammed lived in humble surroundings and did not assume the pomp of power. He, however . . . gave considerable time to his personal appearance. He perfumed his body, painted his eyes, dyed his hair.

Mohammed died in 632 AD. Mohammed

taught that he was no more than one of a line of prophets; but his message was God's final word.

Thus a new religion was founded called ISLAM. Islam is a word which indicates "*submission*" to God. One who submits is called a MOSLEM. There are divisions within Islam, but the vast majority belong to the main body commonly called Sunnites.

**Sunnites
A Sect
Of
Islam**

The Sunnites developed a system with four bases. **First**, the Koran (qur'an) meaning a reading or discourse. These were fragmentary discourses dictated by Mohammed over some 23 years, written on parchment, palm leaves and bones. No collection of these fragments were made until after Mohammed's death. To the non-Moslem, the Koran has no semblance of order and is repetitious. It was soon discovered that the Koran did not deal with many problems the followers faced.

This brought rise to a **second** base, Tradition. The **third** base was Agreement of recognized authorities. The **fourth** base is Deduction by Analogy (*qiyas*).

**Mohammed's
Theology
Of
Heaven**

Much of Mohammed's writings in the Koran tend to run parallel with Bible prophecy. He speaks of resurrections, a falling away in the last days, trumpet blasts and judgments. In Mohammed's heaven, those who die for Allah's cause will reach it, along with the poor, 500 years before the rich. They will recline on couches and be served by handsome youths. They will drink wine from silver goblets and not get drunk.

The Koran, in part, reads:

> By the mercy of Allah,
> there will be no speeches
> at these heavenly banquets;
> instead there will be virgins . . .
> with swelling bosoms but modest
> gaze . . .
> Each blessed male will have
> 72 of these for his reward,
> and neither age nor weariness nor death
> shall mar the loveliness of these
> maidens, or their comrades' bliss
> (lxxviii, 35; xliv, 56, Koran).

Mohammed's Low Esteem Of Women

Mohammed did not hold women in high esteem. The Koran speaks of women as man's supreme calamity, and suspects that most of them will go to hell. Mohammed did, however, put an end to the Arab practice of infanticide (xvii, 31). He also placed woman on the same footing with man in legal processes.

The Koran goes on to say that the wife should recognize the superior intelligence and therefore superior authority of the male (iv, 34).

In Islamic theology, God has given man 104 revelations of which 4 have been preserved: the Pentateuch to Moses, the Psalms to David, the Gospel to Jesus and the Koran to Mohammed. Mohammed preached that the first three have been so corrupted that they cannot be trusted and that the Koran replaces these. He stated that there have been many prophets, but

Mohammed is the last and the greatest (iv, 157). He did, however, admonish his followers to "Consort in the world kindly with Christians" (xxxi, 15).

Five Pillars Of Islam

Modern day Islam has adopted five pillars of practical religion.

1. Recitation of the belief: *"God is the only God; Mohammed is God's messenger."* It is whispered in the ear of the newly born child. It is continually repeated throughout life and should be the last utterance of the dying.

2. Worship is performed five times a day facing Mecca.

3. Legal almsgiving (zakat) is the third pillar of religious duty. It is now largely neglected because of other methods of taxation.

4. Fasting applies mainly to the month of Ramadan which occurs during summer.

5. Pilgrimage is the last pillar of practical religion. This pilgrimage to Mecca must be performed at least once in a lifetime. In this pilgrimage animal sacrifices are made. For three days the pilgrims throw stones at the three pillars in the valley of Mina. Usually, the head is shaved. One who has made the pilgrimage is forever entitled to the honorable title, *"Haj."*

Islam Mushrooming

Today Islam is sweeping the world. It has flooded Great Britain and is making great inroads in the United States. Many Moslems are among the richest people in the world. A large proportion of the world's known reserves of oil is in Moslem territory. They control the largest blocks of wealth. They own many industries, con-

اللّٰهُ اَكْبَر اللّٰهُ اَكْبَر اللّٰهُ اَكْبَر اللّٰهُ اَكْبَر
God is greatest. God is greatest. God is greatest. God is greatest.

اَشْهَدُ اَنْ لَاۤ اِلٰهَ اِلَّا اللّٰه
اَشْهَدُ اَنْ لَاۤ اِلٰهَ اِلَّا اللّٰه
I confess that there is no God but God. I confess that there is no God but God.

اَشْهَدُ اَنَّ مُحَمَّدًا رَسُولُ اللّٰه
اَشْهَدُ اَنَّ مُحَمَّدًا رَسُولُ اللّٰه
I confess that Mohammed   I confess that Mohammed
is the Prophet of God.   is the Prophet of God.

63 beheaded for seizing Great Mosque

Associated Press

RIYADH, Saudi Arabia — Executioners in eight Saudi cities yesterday beheaded 63 of the Muslim zealots who occupied the Great Mosque in Mecca, Islam's holiest shrine, seven weeks ago.

The executions were decreed by King Khaled after the country's religious leaders had issued an edict specifying that attacking the mosque was punishable by death in accordance with the Koran, the Muslim holy book.

Beheading is the customary method of execution in Saudi Arabia and usually is carried out in public. It is believed that the executions were carried out in eight cities in the vast desert kingdom to show that the authorities were in full control of the situation.

Those executed included Juhaiman Bin Seif, the military commander of the fanatic messianic group that attacked the mosque. He was a member of the dissident southern Saudi tribe of Oteiba.

The announcement said that 41 of those executed were citizens of Saudi Arabia. The others were 10 Egyptians, six South Yemenis, three Kuwaitis and one each from North Yemen, Sudan and Iraq. The Saudi government had already said that foreigners had acted out of religious conviction and that no foreign powers were involved in the affair.

The group's leader, Mohammed Bin Abdullah Al-Qahtani, who proclaimed himself the messiah, or mahdi, of the Shiite branch of Islam, was killed during the two-week siege of the mosque by Saudi troops.

The attack on the mosque occurred (See EXECUTIONS on 6-A)

THE RULE OF ISLAM

God has given us all the rules of the game.
—Ayatollah Ruhollah Khomeini

ISLAM IN FERMENT

In Islamic countries, Christians are opposed, prohibited or suppressed. Muslims who accept Christ face separation from their families and are often threatened or even killed by relatives!

trol many banks and own much prime property in the United States. Mohammed's teaching that the rich will reach heaven 500 years later than the poor, does not seem to quench their zeal for gaining wealth in today's world.

The Era Of Khomeini

The Crusaders left a trail of blood in the name of God. The followers of Mohammed are also leaving a trail of blood . . . in the name of Allah. The overthrow of the Shah of Iran in 1979 was maneuvered by an Islamic leader, Ayatollah Ruhollah Khomeini. The name, "Ayatollah," is really a title, and it literally means, *Reflection of Allah"* — *"Ayato—Allah."* On November 5, 1979, Khomeini's forces held about 60 Americans hostage in the U.S. Embassy in Tehran. Their object was to force the extradition of the former Shah of Iran from a New York hospital where he was undergoing treatment for cancer.

Khomeini called the United States "the great Satan, America." Khomeini was a Shiite Moslem. Shiite Moslems consider the "leader" of paramount importance. This movement has political origins and developed among supporters of Ali, who was Mohammed's cousin.

Islam, incorporating some of early Jewish theology, certainly does have a form of godliness . . . but it denies the power thereof.

And God's Word tells us: ". . . *from such turn away"* (2 Timothy 3:5).

13

ZOROASTRIANISM . . . THE RELIGION OF FREE WILL

**Another
Revelation**

About 588 BC, Zoroaster, a religious teacher in Persia (now Iran), claimed to have a *"revelation"* at the age of 30. It is estimated that there are about 10,000 followers of Zoroastrianism left in Iran and about 100,000 in Bombay, India.

Zoroaster (also known as Zarathustra) quite possibly influenced Darius, the Persian King of 522-486 BC. The religion of Zoroaster gradually evolved from a one god system (monotheism) to a two god system. The "Songs" of Zoroaster were placed in a book called the *Avesta*.

Zoroaster claimed he was inspired of God. Zoroaster claimed that he himself guides the righteous over a razor thin, awesome bridge (the Bridge of the Separator) which leads to heaven. The unrighteous fall from this bridge and are guests for all eternity in the House of the Lie.

**A
Strange
Theology**

Yet he believed that Heaven and Hell were not places, but states of existence. After the righteous go to Heaven they must again pass through the Last Judgment. This is an ordeal by fire and molten metal which determines their final destiny.

In later years additional theologies were added to the Avesta. This collection became known as the Gathas.

The ritual of worship includes the burning of a plant . . . the juice of which is considered to be the elixir or immortality. Their confession of faith begins with:

I confess myself a worshipper of Mazdah, a Zoroastrian, a renouncer of the daivas, an upholder of the ahuras.

Daivas are demons and *ahuras* are gods, in this strange religion.

Darius A Follower?

It would appear from some inscriptions found in Iran that Xerxes (486-465 BC), the son of Darius, was a follower of Zoroaster. You will recall that Esther married Xerxes (Ahasuerus) after he set aside Vashti.

During the reign of Artaxerxes (465-425 BC), the Zoroastrian calendar was introduced. The months were named after Zoroastrian divinities. By this time this strange belief had included:

1. Ritual worship of fire
2. Exposure of the dead to be devoured by vultures.

About 650 AD the influence of Islam swept through Iran and the Zoroastrian religion greatly diminished.

The Parsees

Its strongest force now resides in India. They are known as **Parsees** and about 100,000 or so are in the area of Bombay. The Parsees devotedly study their ancient books. They worship fire, earth, water and air as sacred. They expose their dead in "Towers of Silence" for birds of prey to dispose of them.

14

BAHAI . . . A UNITED WORLD RELIGION

**A
New
Deliverer
Arrives**

Far more influential in today's world than Zoroastrianism is another religion coming out of Iran . . . BAHAI.

Mirza Ali Mohammed was the son of a Persian merchant. On May 23, 1844 he claimed to be a manifestation (public evidence or demonstration) of God on earth. He gave himself the title of _Bab_. This is Arabic for "Gate." He predicted that an even greater deliverer would appear and this new deliverer would usher in the dawn of a new age.

This new greater deliverer (following after the _Bab_) was thus to be the Baha-Ullah (Splendor of God). It is strange how these cults pattern so much of their theories on previous religions in their area. While Islam believes that Mohammed was the last and most important prophet . . . Bahai, arriving on the scene some 1200 years later, stated that it has the last prophet! Both religions competed with each other in Iran.

**Bahai
Growing
Worldwide**

Bahai takes its name from the Baha-Ullah. Bahai's are those who accept Baha-Ullah as the *"Demonstration of God"* for this age. Now, over 100 years later, the Bahai faith (which began in Iran) has spread all over the world. The principal writings of this religion have been translated into over 400 languages. The United States, incidentally, is one of the main strongholds of Bahaism.

The Bab claimed that both his mother and father were descendants of the Prophet Mohammed and thus tried to tie into the influence of Islam. Much of the mystery surrounding the Bab occurred when he was taken by Persian authorities at age 30 to be executed.

**The
Mysterious
Execution**

The Bab and a young admirer were suspended by ropes from a nail in the prison yard. The soldiers, 750 of them, aimed their rifles and shot. When the smoke cleared, the Bab had disappeared and the youth was seen alive, unharmed. It was soon discovered that the shots had only severed the ropes. The Bab was found back in his cell. Finally, the Bab was shot and the Bahai historians claim that a gale of dust shrouded the city in darkness for the rest of the day.

The Bahai's declare that God Himself is unknowable. He is only known through manifestations or appearances through prophets. They acknowledge that Jesus, Mohammed, Zoroaster and Buddha are manifestations of God. But they also be-

International headquarters of the Baha'i is on Mt. Carmel in Haifa, Israel. It is the golden-domed shrine of the Bab.

lieve that from 1863 BC on Baha-Ullah became God's spokesman.

Another "Promised One" Arrives

Mirza Hussain Ali declared himself to be the expected Baha-Ullah (Splendor of God). He was born in 1817 at Tehran. The religion suffered a severe setback when two of their group tried to assassinate the Shah of Persia. As a result Mirza was thrown in prison. After his release he travelled to Turkey and then to Baghdad.

It was at Baghdad (in Iraq) that he declared himself "The Promised One." The area where this declaration occurred has been called by Bahai's, "The Garden of Ridvan." Each year from April 21 to May 2 they celebrate the Ridvan Festival.

Baha-Ullah put many of his writings on so-called "Tablets." While imprisoned in Acre (now in Israel), he completed the Kitabi Aqdas which is referred to as The Most Holy Book. It contains the essence of Bahai beliefs.

One World Church

Bahai's believe that there is one God for all mankind and that all religious movements work together for the final "World Order of Baha-Ullah" when mankind will be one.

They strive for a commonwealth of the world . . . a One World idea. They strive for an international system of currency and a unified language. Bahais are forbidden to gamble. They are discouraged from drinking and taking drugs.

They have no clergy and no multi-faceted religious ritual. They meet regularly in a type of social gathering which would resemble a prayer and fellowship meeting.

Their headquarters are at Mount Carmel in Haifa, Israel. Here is located the shrine of the Bab. Just a few miles north, in Acre, is the shrine of the Baha-Ullah.

The chief missionary of the Bahai religion was Abdul-Baha, the eldest son of Baha-Ullah (1844-1921). Abdul-Baha's title was "Interpreter of Baha-Ullah's Teachings." At age 70 he travelled extensively promoting the cause. His areas of travel were primarily in Europe and in the United States.

15

HUMANISM . . . SINISTER, SUBTLE SEDUCTION

**A
Deadly
Philosophy**

Most believers in Christ would have no idea what "humanism" is. I must admit that although I have a college degree and am an author, I really did not take the time to understand the theories of humanism until I reached 53 years of age.

Humanism is a deadly philosophy . . . a philosophy that is often used by Satan to deaden the effectiveness of Christian witness.

Humanism is a system of thought or action that holds that man is capable of self-fulfillment, peace on earth, and right ethical conduct without recourse to God. Humanism therefore is the religion which deifies man and dethrones God.

It has many facets. We see it evident as man attempts to control human life. The acceptance of abortion . . . ending life . . . is a victory for the humanists. Now, extensive studies are going on in what is called "genetic engineering." Genetic engineering is the attempt to control the type of individual that will be born by manipulating the genes.

The Sperm Bank

Already we have witnessed the *"test tube baby"* . . . a baby where sperm and egg were united in a test tube and then implanted in a mother's womb. Plans are already underway in a New York sperm bank to have a genetic supermarket. You go to the sperm bank, tell them the type of child you would like listing such preferences as:

1. Color of hair
2. Color of eyes
3. Short or tall or medium height
4. Race
5. IQ (Intelligence Quotient level)
6. Passive or agressive
7. Career-oriented to Medicine, Engineering, Farming, etc.

Your desires are run through a computer which aligns your specifications with available sperm tubes in the bank. With that match, the wife is implanted with the sperm and conception occurs.

This is just one small aspect of what humanism leads to.

Worships The Creature

Humanism is a doctrine which centers soley on human interests and values. True humanists do not believe in God nor do they, or course, believe in salvation through Jesus Christ nor the existence of a Heaven or Hell. Humanism worships the creature rather than the Creator!

Humanism boasts of **five** basic beliefs in their doctrine:

1. **The Irrelevance of Deity**
   Man's cooperative efforts towards social well-being are of prime importance. God has nothing to do with man's progress or achievements.

2. **The Supremacy of** *"Human Reason"*
   Man alone can think out the answers to the great questions that confront mankind.

3. **The Inevitability of Progress**
   Evolution is the answer to man's salvation. The State is the guardian angel that will control the environment and look after the best interests of man. This leads, of course, to dictatorship.

4. **Science, The Guide to Progress**
   Science itself will be the ultimate provider for mankind. Science will come up with genetic answers to provide a more uniform, manageable population.

5. **The Self-Sufficiency of Man**
   Man is inherently good and is in no need of salvation. Man is autonomous (can function independently) without help from God.

Soon Mercy Killing

Just as humanists were successful in explaining the value of abortion in this *"overpopulated"* world, they will eventually gain their right to institute euthanasia. Euthanasia (*"good-death"*) is specifically causing death by an individual's voluntary action . . . or the action of his loved ones. Eventually, such an accepted practice would cover the *"mercy killing"* of those in nursing homes or those who "have out-lived their usefulness to society." Hitler did this in World War 2.

Such a thought may seem impossible to you. You may not believe that our government would allow such action. But the time will come when it will condone this practice, encourage it, and seek to justify it! Who would have dreamed just a few years ago that abortion would be legalized! The plans of the humanists will be successful until the Battle of Armageddon!

Satanic Work

Many years ago, Dr. L. Nelson Bell, father-in-law of Dr. Billy Graham, wrote:

> . . . within the bounds of the Church, we are witnessing a Satanic work of deception and substitution that is intended to deceive even the very elect. This giant hoax is the substitution of humanism for Christianity.

> . . . Humanism's concern is for material values, but Christianity places spiritual values above all else.

> Humanism is concerned with now, with time and all that occurs in the present. Christianity's eyes are set on eternity, on the city made without hands, eternal in the heavens.

> For the humanist, the "gospel" has to do with man's reconciliation to man; but Christianity's Gospel puts man's reconciliation to God through Jesus Christ above all else.

> The humanist sees "sin" as primarily man's maladjustment to man; for the Christian, sin is disobedience to God's revealed will.

> Humanism is concerned about man's physical, environmental, and material

welfare, but not about his soul.

Christianity recognizes that only as man is reconciled to God can he be properly adjusted to the conditions of everyday life, and that by the presence and grace of God situations that otherwise would be unbearable are often means to draw him closer to God.

Dr. Bell concludes:

The humanist philosophy is a frank statement of the great counterfeit being perpetrated on today's world, one for which many within the Church have fallen.

(from the book, *While Men Slept,* Garden City: Doubleday, 1970), p. 19.

Seeking Utopia Here

Examine those ministries and religious television programs which place emphasis on buildings and the power of positive thinking exclusive of preaching on man's sin and his need of the Saviour! These reflect humanist thinking which seek to capitalize on man's desire for success and wealth and a utopia here and now! They subtly seduce unsuspecting Christians into their camp and rob them of their tithes and offerings which should have gone to worthwhile ministries and missions who faithfully serve the Lord. Oftentimes they use big-name personalities to play on the emotions of the individual, releasing his purse strings, and enlarging their coffers by the millions of dollars!

Examine The Leaders

Watch out for many of those who take up the battle of saving the environment and stage anti-nuclear energy protests. There is nothing morally wrong with being con-

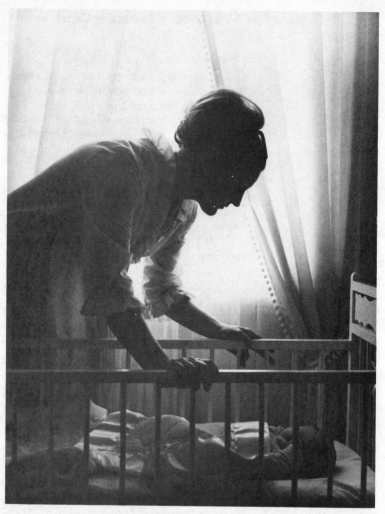

Do you want your child to be taught that Christ did not rise bodily, that Christ is not coming again? Do you want your child to be taught that sin is old fashioned thinking and immorality is acceptable in today's world? That's the path Humanism is taking your children!

cerned about polluting our environment. Nor is it a sin to be against nuclear energy. However, don't follow groups whose leaders are anti-God and anti-family. Look at the leaders of these movements. Their personal life will quickly reveal to you that they are not of God, they are of Satan! Their basic cause is the cause of Humanism!

Many people confuse the words, "humane, humanitarian or humanities" with the doctrine of humanism.

Humane is a quality marked by compassion, by sympathy or consideration for others.

Humanitarian is simply an individual who promotes human welfare and social reform.

A Humanist, however, is anti-God and believes the theology that Man is the Captain of his Ship!

Origin Of Humanism

Humanism basically began in Renaissance Italy (about 1400 AD) when the principal writers of the Middle Ages made a cult of man's human powers.

They revived the works of Plato, Homer, Horace and Cicero and also Dante's *Divine Comedy* which he wrote in 1300 AD.

It is surprising how the aims of humanism and communism are almost identical.

Both deny the supernatural.
Both deny Divine revelation.
Both promote world government.
Both seek to destroy Christianity.
Both seek to control educational system.

'I'm your new watchdog!

They Infiltrate The Schools

It is evident that humanists have been able to gain control of our educational system. Students, who eventually become teachers, are educated for the most part by humanists. The textbooks reflect humanistic evolutionary teaching. Humanism subtly seeps into an individual's thinking through courses that promote humanistic beliefs regarding: history, math, literature, sex education, environmental education . . . even home economics. The humanistic theology is expertly woven into these textbooks of learning.

Communists, of course, admit they are atheists. Humanists simply say they are "non-theists."

The False Teachers

There are false teachers in the Christian church. They may not call themselves humanists. We would know them as liberals or modernists.

1. They deny the virgin birth of Christ.
2. They deny the inspiration of the Holy Scriptures.
3. They deny the atoning, substitutionary death of Christ.
4. They deny the literal, bodily resurrection of Christ.
5. They deny the second coming of Christ.

Paul Blanshard, in his article, *Three Cheers for our Secular State*, writes:

> *I think that the most important factor moving us toward a secular society has been the educational factor. Our schools may not teach Johnny how to read properly, but the fact that Johnny is in school until he is 16 tends to lead toward the elimination of religious superstition. The average American child now acquires a high school education, and this militates against Adam and Eve and all other myths of alleged history.*
> (Humanists magazine, March and April 1976, p. 17)

The Bitter Harvest

Humanism's godless teaching is reaping what it sows! Each year some 10,000 teachers are violently assaulted by their students. It is not unusual for teachers to be injured by their students. In some schools, teachers must wear wrist transmitters that can be used to call for help if a teacher is in danger.

More and more Christian schools are springing up. This, too has become a real threat to humanists. Humanism forces have mounted a well-planned attack on the Christian schools. Almost all 50 states in the United States in unison (armed with federal directives) have pounced legally on various Christian schools to further their humanistic aims. They claim technical *"violations."*

They attempt to control church nurseries, the use of church buildings, the hiring and pay schedules of Christian schools, and the Christian school curriculum.

Humanism is just as deadly as witchcraft or communism . . . perhaps, even more deadly. Humanism is a sinister, subtle seduction that comes in the back door while you are at the front door keeping alert for the enemy! Don't get caught off guard!

Satan has many tricks up his sleeve! Humanism is one of his most effective!

16

WITCHES DON'T RIDE ON BROOMS!

**No
Good
Witches**

When most people think of witches, they may reflect on the Wizard of Oz and the good witch and the bad witch. This is a fairy tale and not true to life.

There is no such thing as a *"good"* witch.

A witch is a woman who claims to have supernatural power by a compact with the devil or evil spirits. Another name is: sorceress.

Witchcraft was forbidden in Israel (Deuteronomy 18:9-14). Witches in Bible days used occult formulas surrounded with mystic mutterings or *"magic"* words. They still do today.

It is interesting to note that the expression translated *"witchcraft"* in Galatians 5:20

(pharmakeia) literally denotes the act of administering drugs and giving of magical potions.

Witchcraft was practiced by Jezebel:

> ... when Joram saw Jehu, he said,
> Is it peace, Jehu?
> And he answered,
> What peace,
> so long as the harlotries
> of thy mother, Jezebel,
> and her witchcrafts are so many?
>
> (2 Kings 9:22)

Condemned By God

Witchcraft was condemned by the prophets, and through Micah, God revealed to Israel that in the future Millennium of 1000 years,

> I will cut off witchcrafts . . .
> thou shalt have no more soothsayers
> (fortune tellers):
> Thy graven images also will I cut off . . .
>
> (Micah 5:12, 13)

Witchcraft was practiced by Manasseh (2 Chronicles 33:6) and abolished during the reign of Josiah (2 Kings 23:24).

Witchcraft, among other things, is the work of the flesh (Galatians 5:20).

Origin In Babylon

Witchcraft had its origins in Babylonian and Assyrian cultures and absorbed their belief in demons and mysticism.

In Babylon there were 53 temples of the great gods, 55 shrines dedicated to Marduk (the chief god of the sun) plus hundreds of other shrines. There were 80 altars alone to the goddess Ishtar (the goddess of love and fertility). The Babylonians, remembered for their Tower of Babel, practiced fortune telling and astrology as well as magic and the casting of spells.

Ancient sorcerers were often necromancers. Necromancy is the practice of claiming to fortell the future by alleged communication with the dead.

Witchcraft, as we know it today, became again popular in the 13th century AD. From the 1200's to well into the 18th century, church and state joined hands to torture and burn witches. Near the end of the 17th century, 55 persons suffered by torture and 20 were put to death in Salem, Massachusetts.

In medieval times a witch was considered to be one who had sold her soul to Satan in exchange for magical powers. Medieval illustrations generally picture the witch as naked and flying through the air on broom handles, generally leaving the house through the chimney.

False Tie With Solomon

In their superstitions, witches met before the throne of Satan who was a goat. One witch would present a child to the demon. Novices were given a black book in exchange for the Gospels which they were renouncing. They were then stripped of their clothes to imitate the nudity of Adam and Eve. It is said that in France alone, under the reign of Charles IX, there were over 100,000 witches.

Much of the black book of sorcery attempts to tie in Solomon with its rites. One is called *La Clavicule de Salomon*. It is interesting that both Islam and Freemasonry also tie in with Solomon. On page 30 of this book is introduced the famous "*magic circle.*" Supposedly, anyone who enters into communication with demons must be enclosed in this circle.

The circle must be nine feet in diameter . . . it must be traced with a consecrated knife, thou shalt make 4 Pentacles (5-pointed stars) with the name of the Creator . . .

In medieval days, professional witches were called upon to prepare **philters,** a potion or charm thought to arouse sexual love or produce a death-spell. It was here that the divining rod had its origin. The divining rod is a forked branch or stick alleged to reveal hidden water or minerals by dipping forward. The words *dowsing* or *witching* are used interchangeably with divining.

In European folklore, the two annual occasions when witches meet are April 30th and October 31st (Hallowe'en).

Organize Into Covens

Practicioners of witchcraft today organize into **covens.** A coven is a group of six male and six female witches with a high priest or priestess. They meet monthly at the time of the full moon. They also meet at eight other occasions they call **sabbats** (the witches' sabbath).

The New York Times described the Hallowe'en sabbat at the home of Raymond Buckland, a Britisher, with a Ph.D. in anthropology. He was one time head of the department of anthropology at Columbia University.

First the witches remove their clothes
   and bathe in salt water to purify
   themselves.
Then, still nude *(sky-clad, as they call it)*
   they descend to the basement
   and step inside a 9-foot circle
   that is drawn about them
   with a 400-year-old sword by
   Mrs. Buckland,
   the high priestess,
   who is known in the craft as
   Lady Rowen.
Once inside the circle,
   the witches sing, chant,
   dance with broomsticks
   in commemoration
   of an ancient fertility rite,
   drink tea and wine,
   and listen to the high priestess read
   from the Book of Shadows.
The ceremony ends after Lady Rowen,
   dressed in only
   a silver crown, bracelet, necklace
   and green leather garter belt,
   takes a horned helmet and
   places it on the head of her husband,
   the high priest,
   who is known as Robat.
This signifies that power
   has been transferred
   from the high priestess
   who reigns during the six months of
   summer,
   to the high priest,
   who rules the six winter months.

John Todd, in relating his experience in witchcraft, attributes his indoctrination into the cult via Raymond Buckland. Witchcraft has its own Bible, called *The Book of Shadows*. This is a compilation of

Failure to follow the Lord always ends in tragedy. "There is a way which seemeth right unto a man but the end thereof are the ways of death" (Proverbs 14:12). Judas found this out. When Saul, faced with a superior enemy and the discouragement of his own army, acted on his own...it led to Endor. This illustration shows Samuel appearing, having been called by the witch of Endor (now called a medium). Saul had previously sinned in deliberate disobedience when he spared Agag and the best of the cattle God had told him to destroy. See 1 Samuel 15:9

rituals and chants which have been drawn from various books of magic.

**Black
Magic**

Witchcraft has been divided by some into **white** magic and **black** magic. Those who practice black magic usually declare openly that they are serving the devil. They are Satan worshippers. Missionaries on the field often come into contact with the evidences of this cult. In Europe much of black magic witchcraft comes from *The Sixth and Seventh Books of Moses*, false magic-type books, which they allege were written by Moses. To possess these books is supposedly to possess the power of Lucifer.

Those who practice white magic declare that they invoke the name of God, not Satan, and they use Biblical phrases. To practice white magic, however, is also to use the name of God and Christ in a manner that violates the Lord's will.

Dr. Merrill F. Unger sums up the distinction between religious white magic and Biblical faith and prayer as follows:

*In biblical faith,
trust is placed solely in the Lord Jesus.
In white magic,
it is deflected
to someone else (the human agent)
or to something else
(one's own faith)
In biblical prayer of faith,
the praying person subjects himself
to the will of God.*

*In white magic
the help of God is demanded
under the assumption
that exercising such power
is in accordance with God's will.
In white magic
the Christian markings are mere
decorations
that camouflage the magical means
for knowledge or power.*

(Merrill F. Unger,
Demons in the World Today, p. 86.)

Richard W. DeHaan writes:

*Biblical faith is built upon trust in God
and expresses itself
in submission to His will . . .
As children of God,
we must remember that we
    "walk by faith, not by sight"
    (2 Corinthians 5:7),
and that the faith that pleases God is
    "the assurance of things hoped for,
    a conviction of things not seen"
    (Hebrews 11:1, KJV).
We must not succumb
to the temptation
to find evidence for our faith
through our senses.*

(Richard W. DeHaan,
Satan, Satanism and Witchcraft, p. 117.)

**Origin
Of
Wicca**

Modern witches refer to their religion as "*Wicca,*" the feminine form of an Old English word meaning *witch*. Wicca draws its membership primarily from the lower middle and middle class people.

In Wicca there are both male and female members but the cult is mainly governed by the high priestess. She is referred to as the Queen of Heaven and her symbols are the moon and stars. Wicca is basically a fertility cult. Witch theology attempts to point out that Christ, with his 12 disciples had an ideal coven with the Virgin Mary as "high priestess."

Garter, Badge Of Office

In modern witchcraft the garter has always been the badge of office of the high priestess. Edward III (1327-1377) openly displayed the garter and acknowledged that he was a witch. He supposedly founded the "double coven" of the Order of the Garter in the witches' honor.

A girdle consisting of three cords and a black-handled knife (athame) is common to all members of a coven.

In the coven ceremony, in the center of their circle stands a small altar, upon which is placed the Book of Shadows, a copy of the liturgy of Wicca, containers for salt and water, a censer, a scourge, a wand, a pentacle (5-pointed star) and a chalice.

Ceremony In The Nude

The naked witches stand just inside the circle with the high priestess at the center, kneeling at the altar. She mixes the salt with the water in a small bowl and then sprinkles this mixture around the outer boundary of the circle and on the heads of the assembled witches.

The nudity of the coven and the Great Rite ceremony, with the ceremonial binding and whipping of the initiate, truly reflect on an immoral group whose origins are definitely satanic.

Anton Szandor La Vey, founder of the Church of Satan in San Francico, performs mystic ceremony. He is author of The Satanic Bible. The root ideas of Satanism go far back beyond the 19th century to the Gnostic sects. The Black Mass is an adoration of the power opposed to Christianity, celebrated over the body of a naked woman. Satanists believe all forms of sexual indulgence are good. They reverse Christian moral values.

One worshiper of witchcraft said:

> The Devil made them believe him to be the true God, and that the joy which the witches had at the Sabbath (sabbat) was but the prelude of much greater glory.

Witches attempted to imitate the church in many ways. The word, Sabbath, was an imitation of the Jewish holy day.

It is estimated that in Great Britain that at least 1 in every 20 persons has some relation with the occult world in one form or another. In the Ozark hill country of the United States, the ceremony of initiating a witch ends with the recitation of the Lord's Prayer backwards!

Growth Of Satanism

Closely aligned with witchcraft is **Satanism.** The root ideas of modern Satanism go far back beyond the 20th century to the Gnostic sects.

The Greek word gnosis means **knows.** The **Gnostic** was not God-centered but, rather, self-centered. Gnostics were very prevalent in the second century. They claimed "to know" the great secrets of religion and life.

Satanists believe that God is evil and the enemy of Satan whose evil is "good." They believe that the Prince of Darkness is the true Lord of Light, Lucifer, "light-bearer."

As this age draws to a close, Satan will once again become very active, with himself and his demons entering human bodies and controlling personalities.

In April, 1966 the Church of Satan formally incorporated in San Francisco. Anton

Szandor LaVey was the founder and *"high priest."* It has been said that he has some 7000 members including a number of celebrities.

It was alleged that Jayne Mansfield was a Satanist and played a large part in the activities of this new Satanic church. Mansfield, a motion picture star of the 1950's and 1960's placed emphasis on her sexual endowments. In June, 1967, while driving with her attorney, she was involved in an auto accident. Both were killed; Jayne Mansfield was decapitated in the collision! In *Man, Myth and Magic*, Volume 23, two pages (3204, 3205) are devoted to this subject. Written by Francis King, the title of this article is: *Jayne Mansfield SATANIST.*

Satan is not dead. He still has great power. It is important that Christians be on the alert, to arm themselves through the reading of God's Word, the Bible, and to pray. Those who fail to abide in Christ on a moment by moment basis may find their effectiveness as a Christian destroyed, should they yield to the Satanic temptation of this age.

No witches do not ride on brooms. They are subtle, friendly; some are even beautiful and enticing. You may find them at your place of employment, in your neighborhood, and perhaps even teaching Sunday School (1 Peter 5:8)!

Be on guard!

For Satan is a master deceiver!

17

THE MYSTICAL ROSICRUCIANS

**The
False
Claim**

This is one of many occult groups which claim to be the guardians of some area of *"hidden knowledge."*

It is built on a legend of Christian Rosenkreuz, founder of the Fraternity of the Rosy Cross.

The Rosicrucians *(rose cross)* cult was begun by Christian Rosenkreuz who was born in 1378 in Germany. He was the son of noble but poor parents. At the age of 5 he was placed in a monastery where he learned Greek and Latin.

As a youth he journeyed to the Middle East and remained for a while at Damascus. At 16 he learned of some *"Wise Men"* at Damcar in Arabia. It is claimed that these wise men warmly welcomed him as a long lost brother. Rosenkruez learned Arabic and was able to translate a secret book, the *Liber M*, into Latin. He spent three years there.

From Damcar he went to Egypt and two years later left for Spain. Disappointed that he was not enthusiastically welcomed in Spain, Rosenkreuz returned to Germany where he began to enlarge his philosopies.

**Three
Monks
And A
Manuscript**

It was there that three monks from his old monastery joined him. They became his disciples. They pledged to keep secret all that they learned from him. However, so that their successors could carry on the Fraternity of the Rosy Cross, they recorded everything in a manuscript book. The monks are listed simply by initials: G.V., I.A., and I.O.

And so this Fraternity of the Rosy Cross began . . . with four members. Eventually others joined: R.C. (his nephew), G.G. and P.D. and finally I.A. and Brother B. All eight members were unmarried and pledged to chastity. They turned out an entire library of books.

With their task completed they decided to go their various ways. They set up a number of guidelines:

1. None of the members were to exercise any profession except that of medicine. They were not to accept payment.
2. No distinctive dress was to be worn.
3. They would meet annually.
4. Each member was to look out for a person worthy to succeed him.
5. The initials R.C. were to be their seal and their password.
6. The identity of the fraternity was to remain a closely-guarded secret for 100 years.

Secret Burial

When the first member died (R.C. Rosenkreuz's nephew), it was decided the burial places of the members should be secret. Soon afterward Rosenkreuz called the remaining six together and supposedly prepared his own symbolic tomb.

Apparently no one knew where or when Christian Rosenkreuz died although he was supposed to have lived until the age of 106. His body was accidentally discovered 120 years after his death when one of the Brothers in the occult order decided to make some architectural alterations in their Temple.

While making his alterations, the Brother discovered a memorial tablet. On the tablet were the names of the earlier members of the Order. He attempted to remove the memorial tablet and in so doing some stones and plaster were broken disclosing a door concealed in the masonry. Upon the door was mystical writing which these Brothers interpreted to read: *"In 120 years I shall come forth."*

The 7-Sided Vault

They entered the vault. It had seven sides and seven corners, each side five feet wide and eight feet high. The sun had never penetrated this tomb but they claimed it was brilliantly illuminated by a mysterious light in the ceiling. In the center was a circular altar. On the altar were brass plates engraved with strange characters.

In each of the seven sides was a small door which, upon being opened, revealed a number of boxes filled with books, secret

Illustration at *left* is the Caduceus. Caduceus is the Latin word for a herald's staff of office. It is associated with the Greek god Hermes, the messenger of the gods. It represents an emblem of power (the wand) combined with wisdom (the snakes).

Symbol at *right* is the Tau Cross. This cross was inscribed on the forehead of every person admitted into the mysteries of Mithras. This symbol is preserved in modern Masonry under the symbol of the T square.

Doubt has always existed as to whether the name *Rosicrucian* came from the symbol of the rose and cross. Some scholars believe this was merely a blind to deceive the uninformed. They state that Rosicrucian is not derived from the flower but from the word *Ros*, which means *dew*. *Ras* means *wisdom* while Rus is translated *concealment*.

Rosicrucians claim that those who join their fraternity will learn the undreamed-of-secrets and wonders concerning the hidden workings of Nature.

instructions and a record of Rosenkreuz's life and travels.

Further investigating, they moved the circular altar and lifted the heavy bronze plate. Much to their surprise they found the body of Christian Rosenkreuz still in a perfect state of preservation. In his hand he held a manuscript copy of *Liber T.*, written with letters of gold on parchment. This manuscript was considered by them their bible. They then replaced the bronze plate on the coffin, closed the door of the vault and sealed it.

This legend was printed in 1615 AD in *Fama Fraternitatis*. This book was soon followed by another that invited the readers to join this brotherhood movement.

The Letter And The Cross

Several other books followed and the story was enlarged upon. It tells a story of Rosenkreuz who on the eve of Easter was meditating when a *"fair and glorious lady"* appeared and delivered a letter, sealed with a cross inviting him to a royal wedding. The next morning he put on white garments, put four roses in his hat and made his way to a castle, being tested along the way.

He witnessed this royal marriage and was invested with the Order of the Golden Fleece, and he discovered the King's secret books of wisdom. The author of this fantasy was Johann Valentin Andreae. Gradually the enthusiasm that this new order had created began to fade.

The Golden Dawn

A by-product of this cult was The Golden Dawn, founded in 1887 by three members of the Rosicrucian Society in England. A clergyman bought some old manuscripts from a bookshop. With the manuscripts was an old letter which said that anyone wanting to decipher the text should communicate with S.D.A. *(Sapiens Donabitur Astris)* through a Fraulein Anna Sprengel. This they did and the Golden Dawn's rituals were written by W.B. Yeats and Mac-Gregor Mathers.

Mathers became increasingly occupied with black magic and sent Aleister Crowley to take over the London lodge. Crowley was violently hostile to Christianity and he saw himself as a new Messiah of a new religion. He eventually came to America.

Enter The Masons

Frank C. Higgens, a modern Masonic symbolist, writes: *"Doctor Ashmole, a member of this fraternity (Rosicrucian), is revered by Masons as one of the founders of the first Grand Lodge in London."* (The Secret Teachings of All Ages, Manly P. Hall, 1928, p. 139).

The Rosicrucians were a secret society based on superstition and occult practices. Most Masons deny there is any link between their fraternity and that of the Rosicrucians. This now brings us to perhaps the most controversial of the current secret societies, the Masons.

18

FREEMASONRY ... ITS SECRETS AND SYMBOLS

Masons Growing

Freemasonry (or Masonry) is the name of one of the largest and oldest fraternal organizations in the world. Its full name is Ancient Free and Accepted Masons.

Masons today say their aims include the promotion of brotherhood and morality among its members. Men of any religious persuasion may join the Masons. Roman Catholics seldom join because it is against church doctrine to do so. Only avowed atheists may not become Masons.

There have been occasions when Masons and Catholics met together. In May, 1978 the Masons and the Knights of Columbus had dinner together in Walla Walla, Washington. It was the first time in Walla Walla history. They fellowshipped on neutral territory at the Elks Club.

Freemasonry has been defined as "*a system of morality veiled in allegory and illustrated by symbols.*"

MASONIC EMBLEMS

32nd Degree Mason

Mystic Shrine

33rd Degree Mason

Master Mason

George Washington, wearing the regalia as a member of the Masons, laid the cornerstone of the United States Capitol in Washington, D.C. in 1793.

**An
Exclusive
Club**

For some, Freemasonry is merely an exclusive club with some secret rituals and camaraderie over a meal. For others, however, Freemasonry's rituals and teachings have a deeper, more spiritual content. Yet Freemasonry is neither a religion nor can it be considered a substitute. Basically it embraces all forms of religion.

Originally the Lodges came into being wherever masons assembled for large scale building works. For a mason to be employed as a professional he was required to know certain passwords and signs that would identify his professional status.

Later the Speculative Freemasons took over. Speculative Masons were those who were not masons by profession but simply a group of men interested in a secret society.

**English
Origins**

In 1717, four fraternal lodges united under the Grand Lodge of England. The Masons of today accept this move as the beginning of their society. The Order quickly spread. It included such famous persons as Benjamin Franklin, George Washington, Frederick the Great of Prussia, Wolfgang Mozart and Voltaire.

**Masons
And
Golden
Dawn**

In 1721, representatives of 16 Lodges commissioned Dr. James Anderson (1684-1739) to prepare a booklet which became known as *Anderson's Constitutions*. Anderson was a minister of the Church of Scotland!

Freemasonry rapidly expanded in Europe. In France a number of the Masonic sects

Interconnected Organizations
AFFILIATED WITH THE MASONS . . .

Presently the number of Masons in the United States is twice that of the rest of the world. About 1 out of every 12 American males is a Mason, according to *World Book Encyclopedia*, 1969 edition, volume 13, p. 210. World membership is in the millions.

Interconnected organizations include:

1. Order of De Molay
An organization of young men between the ages of 14 and 21. Since its founding in 1919, De Molay has initiated more than 2½ million members. Members must be recommended by two chapter members or a senior De Molay or a Master Mason. The De Molay Order was founded in Kansas City in 1919. Its name was taken from Jacques De Molay who was the last Grand Master of the Knights Templars, a famous group of French crusaders. The ritual for the De Molay Order includes secret ceremonies. International headquarters are in Kansas City, Missouri.

2. International Order of the Rainbow for Girls
Another character building organization for girls 12 to 20. Members need not be related to a Mason, but must be recommended by a member of the Masonic Order or of the Eastern Star. The Order has some 275,000 active members.

3. International Order of Job's Daughters
This is for girls 12 to 20 who are relatives of Masons or of persons affiliated with a Masonic organization (called bethels) and an active membership of over 115,000.

4. Order of the Eastern Star
This is a fraternal organization of Master Masons and their wives, widows, mothers, daughters and sisters. It supports charitable projects. It was founded in 1876. The Eastern Star has about 3 million members in 14 countries. Its headquarters are in Washington, D.C.

5. Ancient, Arabic Order of Nobles of the Mystic Shrine
This Masonic order admits members who are at least 32nd-degree Masons in the Scottish Rite or Knights Templar in the York Rite.

6. Daughters of the Nile
Wives of the Mystic Shrine members are members of this exclusive woman's group.

dabbled with magic and occultism. In Germany some were called Order of the Gold and Rosy Cross (Rosicrucians). In England, during the 1880s, the famous magical society, the Mermetic Order of the Golden Dawn adopted most of the Masonic grades.

It is interesting to note that Benjamin Franklin was originally hostile to Freemasonry. However, he did become a Mason in 1731 and remained devoted to the cause until his death in 1790. George Washington was Master of his Lodge when he became the first President of the United States in 1789.

There is no single Grand Master in the United States. Instead there is a Grand Lodge for each State.

The First Rituals

Freemasons meet in an elaborately furnished Lodge room. When a man enters the Masons, he joins a *Blue Lodge*. Members of the Blue Lodge may hold three degrees:

1. Entered Apprentice is the first degree.
2. Fellowcraft is the degree that follows.
3. Master Mason is the third degree.

Each degree in Masonry is supposed to teach a moral lesson. To earn a degree, a Mason must learn the lessons and participate in a ceremony that illustrates them. The Mason can then, after achieving the first three degrees, move on to receive further degrees in either or both of the two branches of advanced Masonry: the *Scottish Rite* and the *York Rite*.

In the *Scottish Rite*, a Mason may advance through 29 more degrees. Thus the first degree of the *Scottish Rite* is actually the fourth degree in Masonry. The highest is the 33rd degree, which is an honorary degree. A 33rd degree Mason is sometimes called *Sovereign Grand Inspector General*.

If a Mason selects to advance in the *York Rite*, degrees include among others, *Mark Master*, *Royal Master* and *Super-Excellent Master*. The three highest degrees are called *Knight of the Red Cross*, *Knight of Malta* and *Knight Templar*. *Knight Templar* is the highest degree in the *York Rite*.

Incompatible With Christianity

On the surface, membership in the Masons would seem like a worthy contribution of time. Much of its work is in the social and constructive realm. Many Masons are members of Bible-believing Churches. They, unfortunately, are unaware of the basic idealogies of Masonry that make it incompatible with Christianity. One cannot serve two masters!

When an initiation ceremony takes place, the one to be iniated removes his tie and jacket and lays aside his money. The symbol here is that Masons accept one regardless of wealth or lack of it.

The Secret Ceremony

He is then led into a room blindfolded. During the course of the ceremony the candidate swears a solemn oath not to reveal Freemasonry's secrets. The blindfold is removed. The candidate is then shown certain handgrips and signs and told certain secret words which are supposed to refer to the symbolical building of King Solomon's temple. He is then presented with a 24-inch gauge and a gavel. The 24-inch gauge represents the 24 hours of the day which are supposed to be divided into prayer, work, refreshment and helping a friend.

Much of Masonry centers around Solomon as the Master Builder. The Masonic legend of the building of Solomon's Temple does not in every particular parallel the Bible version.

Pseudo-Bible Theology

Masonry through its origins and secret rituals seeks to become a religion in the university of life. A man goes through preliminary tests or initiations. He is instructed in the most "sacred," the most secret and supposedly the most enduring of all Mysteries . . . the mystery of SYMBOLISM. Solomon's Temple is intertwined in the myth to give it a quasi-Bible background.

Tarot cards are a set of playing cards bearing pictures of certain traditional allegorical figures and are used in fortune telling. They were used by ancient Egyptians and by Knights Templars from the Saracens. They became a vital element in the Rosicrucian symbolism and had definite Masonic interest as well.

A.E. White, born in 1857 in Brooklyn, made two ventures into ritual magic. He passed through the grades of the First Order in the Golden Dawn occult society. From the wealth of information he picked up he wrote that there are certain indications which point to a possible connection between Masonry and Rosicrucianism. Elias Ashmole (a Rosicrucian) was one of the founders of the first Grand Lodge in London. He was initiated into Freemasonry in 1646.

Dr. Gerard Encausse (better known as "Papus,") studied both magic and occultism. In his book, *Tarot of the Bohemians*, he wrote: "*We must not forget that the Rosicrucians were the Initiators of Leibnitz, and the founders of actual Freemasonry through Ashmole.*"

Ancient Origins Claimed

In several early Masonic manuscripts (Harleian, Sloane, Lansdowne) . . . it is claimed that the craft of initiated builders (Masons) existed before the Flood of Noah's day, and that its members were employed in the building of the Tower of Babel.

A Masonic Constitution dated 1701 refers to Genesis 4:16-24. From the line of Cain (through Methushael) was born Lamech (Genesis 4:18). From Lamech's marriage to two wives (Adah and Zillah) came 4 children: to Adah was born Jabal and Jubal . . . and to Zillah was born Tubalcain and a daughter, Naamah (Genesis 4:20-22).

The Masonic Constitution relates that these four discovered the major crafts of the world (Mathematics, Stonemasonry, iron work and weaving) from Two Pillars of stone. The one stone was called Laturus and the other Marbell.

Two Pillars Of Stone

According to Freemason symbolism, Enoch (son of Cain), erected the two pillars of stone, bearing that all the knowledge of the *"Mysteries"* would be lost at the time of the Flood. Upon the metal columns Enoch supposedly engraved the secret teachings and upon the marble column placed an inscription stating that a short distance away a priceless treasure would be discovered in an underground vault.

Freemasonry theology goes on to say that Enoch was translated from atop Mount Moriah. Such was the pledge to secrecy among ancient freemasonry that Pliny, a Roman writer in the 1st century AD, reveals how one man bit out his own tongue rather than reveal the secrets while in prison.

Three Temples

According to early Masonic teaching there are three Temples of Solomon:

1. The Grand House of the Universe
   in the midst of which sits the sun upon his golden throne.
2. The human body
   which is the Little House made in the image of the Great Universal House.
3. *Soular* House, an invisible structure.

Albert Pike, who studied the mystics, wrote:

> *Freemasonry is more ancient than any of the world's living religions . . . I came at last to see that the true greatness and majesty of Freemasonry consists in its symbols; and that its symbolism is its soul.*

Nesta Webster, in her book, *World Revolu-*

tion, describes alliances between Illuminism (The Illuminati) and Freemasonry. She states that the 1848 French Revolution "*. . . was the second great attempt of illuminzed Freemasonry to bring about a world conflagration.*"[1]

The origins of freemasonry go back many hundreds of years. In a sense, their theology is one of agnosticism.

There is no doubt that Masonic organizations are secret organizations. Their secrecy extends from their special handshake to the many secret code words and symbolism.

As with most secret societies, their origins include lifting of rituals from other secret societies that flourished when Freemasonry began. These origins were certainly not Christian but were based more on humanism and paganism.

There is no doubt that the Masonic Orders endeavor to do good works. Indeed this is part of their program.

A Compromising Position

But a believer in Christ should not be a member of any secret society! This includes Masonic orders! There are many opportunities for a Christian to do good works within the dedicated framework of Christian ministries. To be part of any secret order is compromising your position and greatly lessening your effectiveness in the outreach of the Gospel.

---

[1] Nesta Webster, World Revolution, The Plot Against Civilization (England, Devon: Britons Publishing Company, 1971), p. 157.

Not only that, it is sin!

Christ said in Matthew 5:34, 37,

> But I say unto you,
>   Swear not at all . . .
> But let your communication be
>   Yea, yea;
>   Nay, nay:
> for whatsoever is more than these
>   cometh of evil.

Thus Christians ought not to swear at all, let alone needlessly to fraternal oaths and loyalties — but reserve such loyalty only for Christ. Christ said to give to Caesar what was Caesar's, and to God what was God's (Matthew 22:21). Thus before Caesar (government), we may swear on the Bible in a Court of Law or upon induction into military service. Other loyalties, however, belong to God. He then will at the judgment give forth the true "secrets" (See Revelation 2:17!).

19

THE ILLUMINATI ... REAL OR IMAGINED?

**No
Secrets
Hid
From
God!**

In recent years in Christian circles there have been hushed whispers about the **Illuminati** and their conspiracy to control the world.

Illuminati comes from the root word, *"illuminate."* The basic meaning of *"illuminate"* is

> To give light ... or
> one who is enlightened in mind and spirit.

The Illuminati are defined as *"A people who have or profess to have special intellectual or spiritual enlightenment."*

Satan is a master deceiver. He began as Lucifer, *"Bearer of Light."* The name Illuminati or *"enlightened one"* is derived from this.

**Founding
Of
Illuminati**

The Order of the Illuminati was founded on May 1, 1776 by Dr. Adam Weishaupt. Weishaupt was Professor of Canon Law at the University of Ingolstadt in Bavaria. Weishaupt, although born a Jew, was a convert to Roman Catholicism. He became a Jesuit priest only to break with that order to form his own secret organization. One of the reasons for secrecy was to avoid attacks by the Bavarian Jesuits.

He began his secret order with five members. Each member assumed a secret name. Weishaupt was called Spartacus. (Spartacus was the leader of an insurrection of slaves in ancient Rome. His chief assistant, Herr von Zwack, took on the name of Cato.) Weishaupt hoped to attract the German Freemasons but he was unsuccessful. Finally a few prominent citizens in Munich joined upon learning they would receive the mysterious title of *"Areopagite."*

**Three
Classes
Of
Secret
Society**

In 1779 Weishaupt divided his secret organization into three classes: Novice, Minerval and Illuminated Minerval. Each candidate had to swear an oath to secrecy plus unconditional obedience to Weishaupt. One feature of their society was a most unusual system of mutual espionage. Every member spied on every other member. Each month the Novice had to deliver to Weishaupt a sealed letter which revealed every aspect of his relationship with his superior.

When the Novice was promoted to the Minerval grade a solemn initiation cer-

Adam Weishaupt (left) found the Order of Illuminati in 1776 as a secret organization. Baron Adolph Knigge (right) reorganized the Order along Masonic lines. Eventually he left the Order. Many see Trilateralists as following similar aims.

◆ Thursday, June 22, 1978   Philadelphia Inquirer   9-A

Trilateralists run world —world won't cooperate

By William Greider
Washington Post Service

WASHINGTON — When David Rockefeller's Trilateral Commission came to Washington last week and called upon the Carter Administration, it was like the nest returning to the sparrows.

President Carter, an ex-trilateralist himself, greeted his former brethren in the East Room with praise so generous that it was mildly embarrassing to some.

"I was dumbfounded by some of the things he said," a Trilateral executive said. "I would love to get permission to quote him in our fundraising."

This is terribly off-the-record, like all Trilateral discussions, but Carter told the 200 movers and shakers from America, Western Europe and Japan that if the Trilateral Commission had been in business after World War I, the world might have canceled World War II.

Thus encouraged, the trilateralists heard from three other alumni,

those filling U. S. cabinet posts who count most in global matters—State, Defense and Treasury. A fourth star, National Security Adviser Zbigniew Brzezinski, the intellectual father of the Trilateral idea, canceled his briefing because of illness.

At least 18 top-level executives of the Carter Administration were drawn from the Trilateral membership. So was the foreign minister of Japan. So were the prime minister of France and the labor minister of West Germany. The present membership includes 12 former cabinet officers and top advisers of past U. S. administrations, from Kennedy's to Ford's.

The Trilateral Commission is a very heavy group consisting of bankers and corporate barons, fellow-traveling technocrats, promising politicians and a light sprinkling of trade unionists drawn from three continents.

This has stimulated much spooky theorizing about a Rockefeller shadow on world government, a floating

establishment conspiracy to run everything. In some circles of fervid political imagination, the "Trilateral connection" is shorthand for puppets on a string, responding to a secret agenda.

The reality, alas, is less dramatic. On paper, they run the world. But, in the flesh, the trilateralists get together and mostly talk about how the world ought to be run, if only the world would cooperate.

This humble little secret slipped out from under the mirror-paneled doors at L'Enfant Plaza Hotel here, where the trilateralists met for three days last week: The heavyweight members, despite their awesome economic clout, feel defensive, uneasy, unloved.

'A rich man's club'

"It's surprising," said one participant, "that these big, powerful, hefty tycoons would be so defensive. They are not terribly confident."

emony was performed. The Novice was taken at night to a dimly lit room. Here he learned certain secret signs and a password. He was allowed to know who else was in his Minerval grade but the identities of the Illuminated Minerval were not disclosed.

**The
Ultimate Aims**

By the time a member had reached the grade of Illuminated Minerval, he learned the ultimate aims of the Order:

1. Abolition of all ordered government
2. Abolition of private property
3. Abolition of inheritance
4. Abolition of patriotism
5. Abolition of all religion
6. Abolition of the family (via abolition of marriage)
7. Creation of a World Government

Weishaupt wrote to his chief assistant, Cato: *"The most admirable thing of it all is that great Protestant and reformed theologians (Lutherans and Calvinists) who belong to our Order really believe they see in it the true and genuine mind of the Christian religion. Oh man, what can not you be brought to believe?"*

**Luring
The
Unsuspected**

He knew how to lure unsuspecting people into his organization and once wrote: *"These people swell our numbers and fill our treasury; get busy and make these people nibble at our bait . . . but do not tell them our secrets. They must be made to believe that the low degree that they have reached is the highest."*

Thus it was that influential people of that day became Novices, but these never attained to the higher grades where the real aims of the Illuminati were known.

Infiltrating Freemasonry

Weishaupt gradually infiltrated the Freemasons. On July 16, 1782 at the Congress of Wilhelmsbad, an alliance between Illuminism and Freemasonry was finally sealed. On that day the leading secret societies were infiltrated, and to some degree, united . . . more than 3 million members!

The most influential member of those who then became Masonic Illuminati was Baron Adolph Knigge (1752-96). He assumed the pseudonym, Philo. He was a first class organizer. Johann Goethe, the famous German poet and dramatist was among those that joined at that time. Knigge quarrelled with Weishaupt because of his anti-clerical stand and left the Order.

Eventually the Bavarian government banned both the Illuminati and the Freemasons on March 2, 1785. Weishaupt was forced to leave the country. The Bavarian government heard four leading members of the Illuminati testify before a Court of Inquiry exposing the Satanic nature of its aims. A voluminous array of documents were found in Illuminati headquarters. The Bavarian government published them to warn all the other countries of Europe. The name of this document was: *Original Writings of the Order and Sect of the Illuminati.*

Illuminati Arrives In America

However, by this time 15 lodges of the Order of the Illuminati had been established in the 13 Colonies. This was before the Colonies were united and the Constitution adopted. In 1785, the Columbian Lodge of the Order of the Illuminati was established in New York City. Its members included Governor DeWitt Clinton, Clinton Roosevelt and Horace Greeley. A Lodge in Virginia was identified with Thomas Jefferson.

In 1797, Professor John Robison published *Proofs of a Conspiracy*. He warned the world of Illuminati infiltration into Masonic Lodges.

Strange Bedfellows

An English woman, Frances "Fanny" Wright, came to New York in 1829 to give a series of lectures promoting the Women's Auxiliary of the Illuminati. She advocated the entire Illuminati program including Communism. She also spoke of equal opportunity and equal rights, atheism, free love and the emancipation of women. Clinton Roosevelt (an ancestor of FDR), Charles Dana and Horace Greeley were appointed to raise funds for this new undertaking.

Clinton Roosevelt wrote a book, *Science of Government*. In it he wrote: ". . . there is no God of justice to order things aright on earth; if there be a God, he is a malicious and revengeful being, who created us for misery."

Adam Weishaupt died in 1830 at the age of 82. It is believed he rejoined the Catholic Church with a death-bed repentance.

The Order of the Illuminati was revived in Berlin in 1906 by Leopold Engel, at the request of Theodor Reuss. Reuss was engaged in several pseudo-Masonic activities.

Weishaupt was just another link in a continuous chain who sought to perpetuate secret societies for their own evil ends. There are many conspiracies to undermine Christianity. To point to the Illuminati as the singular moving force would be to attach to it something that has no convincing foundation. Long before Adam Weishaupt was born, the symbol he incorporated (The All-Seeing Eye) had its origin in Babylon days.

There is a single force which seeks to destroy the world. The Order of the Illuminati is simply one of its servants. That force is Satan who was the Angel of Light, Lucifer.

20

THE ILLUMINATI AND THE ALL-SEEING EYE

**The
Pyramid
And The
Dollar**

Dr. Adam Weishaupt, founder of the Order of the Illuminati adopted the All-Seeing-Eye symbol at the time he founded his Order on May 1, 1776. The symbol is a pyramid with its top triangular stone being an eye.

This symbol is found on the back of a $1 United States bill. At the base of the pyramid is the date 1776. Many, in error, believe this refers to the date of the signing of the Declaration of Independence. This is not solely true. It refers also, according to many, to the date Weishaupt founded the Order of the Illuminati.

Although the pyramid on the American dollar with its 13 levels ties in with the 13 colonies, the original association was with ancient Egyptian and Babylonian mysticism. Thus, mystery surrounds the implications found in the Great Seal of the United States of America.

The Big Brother All-Seeing Eye

Note also that the cornerstone is missing from the top of the pyramid. In its place is the All-Seeing-Eye. Weishaupt's mutual spying system was an integral part of his program to keep his associates in line. The eye symbolized a Big Brother controlling his domain. Those who dismiss this idea say the eye in the Great Seal is the *"all-seeing"* eye of God. However, the words in Latin underneath the pyramid of the Great Seal (Novus Ordo Seclorum) mean *"New Secular Order."* The words in Latin above the Great Seal (Annuit Coeptis) mean *"Announcing the Birth."* Put the two together and you get *"Announcing the birth of a New Secular Order."*

With the cornerstone supplanted by an all-seeing eye, any reference to Christ is absent. In Ephesians 2:20 God's Word reveals:

Jesus Christ Himself . . .
the chief corner stone.

And in Mark 12:10 and Luke 20:17, Christ is described as:

The Stone which the builders rejected.

Designs Behind The Great Seal

Who was appointed to prepare The Great Seal of the United States of America? On July 4, 1776 Thomas Jefferson and John Adams (both Masons) and Benjamin Franklin (a Rosicrucian) were commissioned to design the seal. This occurred some 31 years before John Adams became aware of the Illuminati conspiracy.

At the time that the United States of America was founded, European mysticism was not dead. Careful analysis of the Great Seal disclose a mass of occult and Masonic symbols. One such symbol is the so-called American Eagle. In its initial Seal, the Eagle was actually the Phoenix bird, which resembles closely the Eagle.

The Egyptian Phoenix was represented as having the body of a man and the wings of a bird. The Phoenix was a symbol of regeneration. Its third eye had an occult function which was known by the ancient priesthood. The Phoenix, in mythology, was reborn out of its own dead self seven times seven. The Phoenix was a symbol also used by the Rosicrucians. In the Grand Rosicrucian magic formula the pyramid is the center of its design and the phoenix also appears.

Napoleon and Caesar's zodiacal eagle of Scorpio are really Phoenixes. It is interesting to note that the All-Seeing-Eye of the Illuminati is also seen in the meditation room of the United Nations in New York. No one for certain can say that the Great Seal of the United States was created by those whose minds were evil. However, a great weight of evidence points to the fact that the Rosicrucians exerted tremendous influence in its creation. And the Seal does have occult significance.

The top illustration is the bird's head from the first Great Seal of the United States in 1782. The bottom illustration is the Great Seal of 1902. The bird in the first Seal bore little resemblance to that of the eagle. This first so-called eagle resembled the mythological phoenix of antiquity. The phoenix bird was the Egyptian symbol of regeneration. Thus, the new country (United States) rising out of the old (Great Britain).

21

ILLUMINATI INFLUENCE IN THE UNITED STATES

**Rise
Of
Karl Marx**

After Adam Weishaupt died, Giuseppe Mazzini (an Italian revolutionary leader) was appointed as Director of the Illuminati. He held this position from 1834 to 1872. Shortly after Mazzini took control of the Illuminati an obscure intellectual joined one of the branch organizations of the Illuminati called the League of the Just. His name was Karl Heinrich Marx.

Karl Marx denounced his Jewish birth and the Christianity of his parents, who were converts. He thus embraced Athiesm, and studied at the universities of Bonn and Berlin and planned to be a professor of history and philosophy. He wrote the book *Das Kapital* which became the bible of the Communist movement. He wrote it with the help of Friedrich Engels.

Marx had a sad personal life . . . much of it due to his own failures. His marriage resulted in six children. Three of his children died of starvation while infants. Two of his children committed suicide.

It was in 1847 that Marx came to write what later became known as the *Communist Manifesto*. A manifesto is a public declaration of motives and intentions. This book outlined the overall plans for the future which urged laborers to revolt and for the government to own all property. Marx was such an unknown at that time that his name did not even appear on this document until 20 years after it was first published.

The Communist Manifesto

The *Communist Manifesto,* which struck out at capitalism was basically simply a rehash of the writings of Adam Weishaupt and his disciple, Clinton Roosevelt.

In this same period, Giuseppe Mazzini selected Albert Pike to head the Illuminati activities in the United States.

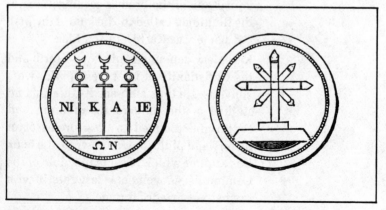

Symbolic cross emblems above were Standards of the pagan nations of the East.

Albert Pike was born in Boston in 1809. He went to Harvard and later served as Brigadier-General in the Confederate Army. Albert Pike was a genius who used his intelligence with evil intent. He could read and write in 16 ancient languages.

Admirer Of Cabala

He was an admirer of the secret Hebrew cult of Cabala (*Qabbalism*). Pike at that time was head of the Ancient and Accepted Scottish Rite of Freemasonry. Mazzini, in a letter dated January 22, 1870, wrote to Pike:

> *We must create a super rite,*
> *which will remain unknown,*
> *to which we will call*
> *those Masons of high degree*
> *whom we shall select.*
>
> *With regard to our brothers in Masonry,*
> *these men*
> *must be pledged to the strictest secrecy.*
> *Through this supreme rite,*
> *we will govern all Freemasonry*
> *which will become*
> *the one international center,*
> *the more powerful*
> *because its direction will be unknown.*

This letter was published in the book, *Occult Theocrasy* by Lady Queenborough, pages 208-209.

Pike And His Councils

This secret organization was established by Pike under the name of The New and Reformed Palladian Rite. Supreme councils were founded in Charleston, South Carolina, in Rome and in Berlin.

Palladism is the cult of Satan in the inner

shrines of a secret ritual to surpass all other secret rituals.

Albert Pike's most famous book is the 861 page *Morals and Dogma of the Ancient and Accepted Scottish Rite of Freemasonry*. It was published in 1871. In it, he writes:

*The blind Force of the people
is a force that must be economized,
and also managed . . .
it must be regulated by intellect.*

*When all Forces are combined, and
guided by the Intellect (the Illuminati),
and regulated
by the Rule of Right and Justice . . .
the great revolution
prepared for by the ages
will begin to march.*

*It is because Force is ill regulated,
that revolutions prove failures.*

(Morals and Dogma, pp. 1, 2)

Symbol at *left* is the Crux Ansata, sometimes called the Onk. It combines the masculine Tau Cross with the feminine oval to symbolize the principles of generation. Illustration at *right* is Egyptian conception of creation. Much of this symbolism has continued through Freemasonry and other secret organizations.

On July 14, 1889 he issued this statement to the 23 Supreme Councils of the world:

That which we must say to the crowd is:
  We worship a God,
  but it is the God one adores
  without superstition.

To you,
Sovereign Grand Instructors General,
we say this, that you may repeat it
to the Brethren
of the 32nd, 31st and 30th degrees:
  The Masonic religion should be,
  by all of us
  initiates of the high degrees,
  maintained in
  the purity of the Luciferian doctrine.

In 1871 Giuseppe Mazzini issued a remarkable letter in which he graphically outlined plans for three world wars. Until recently this letter was on display in the British Museum Library in London.

Pike aided in making this plan known in the United States. It was a blueprint for three wars!

22

THE THREE WARS—PLANNED OR COINCIDENCE?

**An
Interlocking
Conspiracy**

Albert Pike's three Supreme Councils controlled 23 other subordinate groups throughout the world.

The Mazzini-Pike plan was to control the world. How would this be accomplished?

The plan was relatively simple. It called for, according to the writings of some, Communism, Fascism, and the struggle for the Mid-East to foment three global wars and at least two major revolutions.

**World
War
1**

The First World War was to enable Communism to destroy the Czarist government of Russia and replace it with militant atheism. This came to pass and we now see the results of this overthrow.

World War 2

The second war would begin by manipulating the governments of Great Britain and Germany to start a world war. Hitler, however, accomplished this almost single handed, bringing on World War 2. After this war, Communism would then be in a position to destroy other governments and weaken religions. This also came to pass. Russia controls most of Europe and the Gospel has been effectively suppressed in many nations. This atheistic movement has also successfully spread to China when China became closed to Christianity after World War 2.

World War 3

The Mazzini-Pike blueprint also called for a World War 3. This would begin by firing up the controversy between Judaism and the Moslem world. They hoped that the Zionists and Moslems would destroy each other and bring the rest of the world into a final conflict. This Armageddon would bring complete social, political and economic chaos.

While the Illuminati secret few may fan the fires, it must be seriously questioned how much world influence this group has had in the last century. It is quite possible that these Illuminati schemes for 3 World Wars are more recent inventions, post-dated to give authenticity to those who seek to blame the sin and suffering of today's world on some secret few.

In any event, to fill the void created by Armageddon would come a World Government, headed by the Illuminati. In a letter now catalogued in the British Museum in London, Pike wrote to Mazzini:

Then everywhere,
    the people,
    disillusioned with Christianity,
will receive the true light,
    that will follow
    the destruction of Christianity
    and atheism,
both conquered and exterminated
at the same time.

The Illuminati are against both Christianity and atheism and seek to destroy both and supplant it with Satan as their god whom they call, Lucifer. In fact they do not accept the doctrine of Satanism.

Believers can look for greater persecution in the years ahead. Many Christians may become martyrs because of their testimony for Jesus Christ. See Revelation 20:4.

**Lucifer
Theology**

In the Illuminati doctrine, Lucifer is God and the doctrine of Satanism is a heresy. Lucifer is their God of Light. The Christian God (Adonay), they state is the God of Evil.

What about World War 3? If you carefully read current news events and see the alignment of nations it is not hard to understand that the third World War could be between forces united with Israel against the forces united with Communism and Islam.

Satan's Prophets

Perhaps the Illuminati, in league with Satan as they are, actually (even without realizing it) have had revealed to them Satan's program in advance? If so, they have truly been Satan's prophets of coming doom!

**Overthrow
In
Iran**

The sudden overthrow of the Shah of Iran in early 1979 certainly changed the course of history. Ayatollah Ruhollah Khomeini, who took control of Iran, is a political, religious leader who knew how to whip up violently strong anti-Israel feelings. His hatred to the Jew even extended to acts of violence against the United States.

Scripturally speaking, the plan of Satan is to weaken the nations of the world and set up his own kingdom here on earth (Isaiah 14:12-15).

God's Word does tell us that at the end of the age Satan would set nation to war against nation and kingdom against kingdom (Matthew 24:6, 7). More changes have been made in alignments of nations in the last 10 years than have occurred in many centuries.

Satan's Plan Revealed

We are living in the Last Days just prior to the Rapture. God's Word, the Bible, does reveal to us that part of Satan's plan would include the rise of Communism, a suppressive anti-God power in Russia. Ezekiel 38:1 to 39:16 does tell us that Russia will align with four Islamic (Moslem) nations and invade the tiny nation of Israel. Daniel 11 also supports this as does the prophecies in the book of Revelation.

Start Of World Government

Satan will set up a world governmental system, appoint his own ruler over it. This world dictator in Scriptures is called the Beast and is also known as Antichrist. He will have a pseudo-religious assistant who is known as the False Prophet. Everyone will be commanded to worship Satan as the supreme god of the universe. The False Prophet will direct everyone to display a mark of allegiance either on their right hand or on their foreheads (Revelation 13:16, 17).

YOUR SOCIAL SECURITY NUMBER

Says an official report: "The number has become vital to record-keeping in a number of federal agencies . . . Depending on where you live, you may find it on your local tax form, your bank account, your library card—even your dog's license-tag application."

Satan's kingdom on earth is vividly described in Revelation 13:4-8. And at the end of this brief reign of this Satanic world dictator, the armies of the nations will gather in Israel in the world's greatest battle, the Battle of Armageddon!

The only thing that is preventing the establishment of Satan's government over every nation today is the Holy Spirit. Many Christians are still standing up and counting for Christ, witnessing of salvation through Him.

The 7-Year Tribulation Period

In the 7-year Tribulation Period, the centuries-old dream of the Illuminati will reach its goal . . . though only temporarily. For the Illuminati, as all other secret societies and evil political movements are controlled by Satan. They are his visible ambassadors. They, along with his invisible ambassadors (Satan's angels), will have a 3½ year period (the second half of the 7-year Tribulation) to shower terror and tyranny over the entire world. It will be at that time that their true nature will be known and revealed. No longer operating in secret, the smell of victory will rage over the nations.

BUT, GOD!

And that's what makes the difference. You see, Satan is already a defeated foe! And he knows it!

The Downfall

The downfall of the Satanic conspiracy is described in 2 Thessalonians 2:7-9. The Illuminati (the Light Bearers) will finally be defeated by the true Light of the World,

Jesus Christ when He comes in His brightness at the Battle of Armageddon at the end of the 7-year Tribulation Period!

How important it is for believers to:

> ... *Put on the whole armour of God,*
> *that ye may be able*
> *to stand against the wiles of the devil.*
>
> *For we wrestle*
> *not against flesh and blood,*
> *but against principalities,*
> *against powers,*
> *against the rulers*
> *of the darkness of this world,*
> *against spiritual wickedness*
> *in high places.*
>
> *Wherefore,*
> *take unto you the whole armour of God,*
> *that ye may be able*
> *to withstand in the evil day,*
> *and having done all,*
> *to stand."*
>
> (Ephesians 6:10-13)

You are fortunate to be standing on the threshold of God's great tomorrow. The forces of Satan may be all around you. But remember, Satan is a defeated foe!

For greater detail on Antichrist and the 7-year Tribulation Period, we suggest you read: **GUIDE TO SURVIVAL** by Salem Kirban ($4.95) and **THE RISE OF ANTICHRIST** by Salem Kirban ($4.95). Salem Kirban, Inc., 604 Mason's Mill Road, Huntingdon Valley, Penna. 19006. Add $1 to cover postage.

23

THE FABIAN SOCIETY AND ITS SINISTER SEDUCTION

An
Evil
Aim

In 1884 the Fabian Society was founded in England with a secret aim to create a classless, socialistic society. Lenin's Bolsheviks made their entry about this time as well.

Both groups had similar utopian basic aims but employed different methods to achieve their goals. The Bolsheviks (now known as Communists) seek to control the world through violent, revolutionary means.

The Fabians, however, teach that socialism can be achieved, gradually, through a series of reforms. Their theology is known as Socialism. The Fabian Society was named for Quintus Fabius Maximus, a Roman general who avoided defeat by refusing to fight any decisive battles against Hannibal.

**The
Sinister
Seduction
Of
Gradualism**

Thus the Fabian strategy is one of grad-ualism. **Gradualism** is the principle of seeking to achieve political changes or goals gradually. One is reminded of the frog who is placed in a cool kettle of water on a stove. The frog has no fear. The water is gradually heated so slowly that the frog does not notice the temperature changes. He is lulled into comfort of a false security until it is too late!

We are guilty of being pawns in the game of gradualism. For an example, take the price of gasoline. Undoubtedly you can remember when a few years ago gasoline sold for 39¢ a gallon (or cheaper!). When the price soared to 67¢ a gallon, you rushed to the gas station that was selling gas at 59¢ a gallon and thought you were getting a bargain. When it soared to over a $1 a gal-lon, you thought 99¢ a gallon was cheap!

Therefore, by gradualism, your yardstick for accepting what was and was not a bar-gain was warped. Actually 99¢ a gallon is not cheap when you compare it to 39¢ a gallon. But through gradualism you have fallen into the trap of accepting higher prices and considering them bargains.

Television is the same way. In its infancy, television programming was clean and wholesome. Within a few short years the sinister forces of Satan infiltrated. Grad-ually a few curse words were allowed "in their context." This paved the way for what is now considered by many X-rated television on all 3 major United States networks.

Abortion followed the same pattern . . . gradualism. It was not too long ago that abortion was illegal. Today it is a way of life done millions of times each year by respected doctors in accredited hospitals. **GRADUALISM.**

So it was that the Fabian Society realized the basic fault in man . . . that he was highly susceptible to invasion of new ideas . . . via gradualism!

Towards A New World Order

Writers George Bernard Shaw and H.G. Wells and social reformers Sidney and Beatrice Webb were among early members of the Fabian Society. In England, Fabian leaders joined the Labor Party. They did not believe in class conflict but were convinced that gradual measures would in due time bring about a socialist state. It did!

The Fabians worked for a new world order. They did this by indoctrination of young scholars. These intellectual revolutionaries, they believed, could gain power in the various policy making agencies of the world and thus achieve the aims of the Fabian Society. Their tactics became known as the *"doctrine of inevitability of gradualism."*

From ancient times, political philosophers knew that the most effective way to conquer a man is to capture his mind.

Originated With John Ruskin

The Fabian Society was a natural outgrowth of what John Ruskin had been promoting for years in England. John Ruskin (1819-1900) taught at Oxford and advocated a utopian-type society. In one of his statements, he reveals his theory when he said:

> My continual aim has been
> to show the eternal superiority
> of some men to others,
> sometimes even of one man to all others.

Much of Ruskin's theories came from Plato, whom he worshipped. There is a remarkable parallel in the writings of Ruskin, Marx and other followers of Plato.

Plato's ideal society included the following:

1. The elimination of marriage and the family.
2. All men would belong to all women.
3. Children resulting from these promiscuous unions would be taken over by the government, as soon as they were weaned. They would be raised anonymously by the state.
4. Women would be equal with men.
5. Women would be expected to fight wars with men and perform labor like men.
6. Selective breeding of men and women would take place under government control.
7. Children considered inferior or crippled, in this breeding process, would be destroyed.

3-Level Society

Plato advocated a three-level structure of society: the ruling class, the military class, the worker class.

Now, remember Plato did not live in the 20th century! He was a Greek philosopher who lived at the beginning of the 4th century BC (427-347)! Yet what he describes as the "ideal" society is on the verge of being fulfilled today!

Plato's philosophy was patterned, in part, from Pythagoras, a philosopher of the 6th century BC. The school of Pythagoras was a communistic aristocracy; men and women pooling their goods, educated together, and offering themselves as guardian rulers of the state.

**A
Continuous
Line**

Why all this ancient history? By studying the origins of satanic influences, one can trace the continuous line of people or groups or world rulers who knowingly (or unknowingly) became pawns in a conspiracy of power.

John Ruskin could be considered the Plato of his day. One of Ruskin's students was Cecil Rhodes (1853-1902). Rhodes became a firm believer in the Ruskin theology.

**Rothschilds
And
Rhodes**

With financial support from Lord Rothschild, Cecil Rhodes was able to monopolize the diamond mines of South Africa. Rhodes became a millionaire. Much of his money went to start the Rhodes Scholarships at Oxford. It was his desire to unite the world under a central government. And on February 5, 1891, Cecil Rhodes formed a secret society.

These men could not be considered evil geniuses, as some mentioned in this book. These, rather were men who thought that world peace and harmony could be brought into being by their creating world organizations for good. Some, however, had other uses for these world leagues!

Many of the members of this secret society were devoted disciples of John Ruskin. In this secret society, Rhodes was the leader. Among those who were to be included in the "Circle of Initiates" was Arthur (Lord) Balfour and Lord Rothschild. There was to be also an outer circle known as the "Association of Helpers." This was later called the "Round Table Organization."

The Round Table

This secret society gradually extended into other countries and in 1910 began publication of a quarterly magazine, **The Round Table.** Among their chief supporters were members of the Astor family.

Their desire was to have the capital of this world federation in the United States. Institutes of International Affairs were established worldwide, including the United States where it is now known as the Council on Foreign Relations.

24

THE MONEY MANIPULATORS GREED FOR POWER

**The Five
Largest
U.S. Banks**

It is not a sin to be wealthy. The 5 largest commercial banking companies in the United States are (in the order of assets):

1. BankAmerica Corporation (San Francisco)
2. Citicorp (New York)
3. Chase Manhattan Corporation (New York)
4. Manufacturers Hanover Corp. (New York)
5. J.P. Morgan & Company (New York)

What does become sin is the **love** of money (1 Timothy 6:10). In fact God's Word tells us that the love of money is the root of all evil! Such a love has drawn Pastors out of the pastorate. Such a love has caused believers to warp their priorities, giving the Lord second best.

To those who do not know Jesus Christ as personal Saviour and Lord, the love of money spawns a multitude of evils and becomes Satan's playground! Wealthy, independent people, seek to hold public office . . . devoting all their energies day and night to become elected . . . not, however for money alone. They have greedily gained money and have still not found happiness. Now they seek what they believe is the next ultimate — **POWER!**

If you are an astute Christian you can see these forces at work in our cities, in our states, in our federal government and in the world. Some have alleged that the five banks we have listed at the beginning of this chapter are powerful international dynasties able to wield great power. The Rockefellers have been closely associated with Chase Manhattan and appear on interlocking directories of some of the world's largest corporations. It has been alleged that members of the Rockefeller family had a great deal of influence in setting up the Shah and with him Iran as a powerful oil country . . . and that this manipulation triggered the overthrow by Ayatullah Khomeini and the subsequent holding of American hostages. Indeed, the Shah himself counter-claimed that he was overthrown because he *"stopped paying off the religious leaders!"*

**Are
We
Bankrupt?**

We may already be living in the age of Antichrist! **He may already be alive on earth!** It is my opinion that the United States is becoming bankrupt! It is becoming bankrupt financially! It is becoming bankrupt morally! It is becoming bankrupt spiritually! And like Israel of old . . . it has become hardhearted and stiffnecked. And like Israel of old . . . it will someday suffer complete collapse . . . controlled by Antichrist! That's my prediction.

Economically, we have spent money we don't have and then printed more money to make up for the deficit. The federal debt increased more during the 1970's than in the entire previous history of the United States!

Federal Debt Astronomical!

In 1970, the Federal debt was 396 Billion dollars! In 1979 the interest on the debt alone was 50 Billion dollars a year! This was almost one-half of the 1979 defense budget!

Such spending places the United States at the mercy of those who control the wealth of the world. It would not be surprising to learn that these money manipulators first created the situation that weakened the United States so they could finally control this great nation! And why not? Is it not in the United States where we have the greatest expansion of the Gospel? Is it not in the United States where Bible-believing ministers are on more television stations than the large network talk shows? This offends Satan. So naturally the United States will be one of his prime areas of attack, and he will use the money manipulators to breed hate and to put the power into the hands of a few, demon-possessed individuals! My present personal belief is that Antichrist will emerge from the United States!

It may surprise you to know that the United States is now controlled, in a large part, by foreign interests! In 1970, foreign holdings in the United States came to only $11 Billion. In 1975, foreign holdings in the United States came to $60 Billion. By 1980, foreign holdings in the United States have soared to over $125 Billion!

Strange Turnaround

The largest creditor in 1980 to whom the United States owes money is WEST GERMANY! Japan runs a close second. Yet, here are two nations who we fought against in World War 2! In 1980 the Middle East countries had over at least $15 Billion invested in the United States. In hidden assets this figure could be much, much higher.

Another surprising fact is the strange, swift growth of foreign banks in the United States. In 1975 the United States assets of foreign banks was about $25 Billion. Just five years later, by 1980, this had soared some 300% to assets of almost $100 Billion (while U.S.-owned banks only had a 64% gain)!

Right now almost 20% of all big U.S. business loans are made by foreign banks! It is easy to see how the United States can be manipulated by foreign powers with money barons in the United States acting as their agents. The answer is not simply placing a Christian President in office. He is no match for the money manipulators who call all the plays! We recognize that God is in control! We also recognize that God warned us that we are living in the last days when perilous times would come (2 Timothy 3:1).

Misplaced Blame

There is no easy answer to the problems of today. Some, again looking for a scapegoat, would blame all the problems of the world on the Jews. The Jews are blamed for the Federal Reserve system, the Illuminati, Hitler and even for the Iranian crisis of 1979. They are also blamed for the oil shortage! One might think that the Jews were the only sinners in need of the Saviour!

In the Middle Ages the Jewish people were denied Guild membership in manufacturing arts and thrust into banking and merchant lines. These two proved in years to come to be most profitable. In this way, through persecution, the Jewish people have had an uncanny ability to make money and accumulate wealth. God has blessed them with financial prudence . . . just as Germans are blessed with fine craftsmanship and Japanese with electronic ingenuity.

No, true Christians realize that the Jews are not to blame for the ills of the world. The real problem began thousands of years ago when sin entered the world through Satan. It was when Lucifer, the angel of light, not satisfied with his exalted position in Heaven . . . sought POWER!

And that's today's problem, for the most part . . . the POWER PERSUADERS to use money as their club to gain control of the world system! There is nothing that they would like better than a One-World system. The United States is drifting to this position. Right now through government hand-outs of one kind or another, approximately 60% of the people in the United States depend on the United States for their welfare!

**The
Federal
Reserve**

Now what about the Federal Reserve System? It is neither Federal, nor Reserve!

Louis T. McFadden, who, for more than 10 years, served as Chairman of the Banking and Currency Committee, is reported to have said on the Floor of the House of Representatives:

> We have in this country
> one of the most corrupt institutions
> the world has ever known.
> I refer to the Federal Reserve Board
> and the Federal Reserve Banks . . .
>
> They are not Government institutions.
> They are private monopolies
> which prey
> upon the people of these United States
> for the benefit of themselves
> and their foreign customers.[1]

This may or may not have been the case at one time. Today's Federal Reserve Board does not outwardly seem to be a group of world criminals, but rather a group of responsible bankers attempting to manage the money of the United States at a desperate time. So much power, however, exists here that there is always the potential for the wrong group to gain control of this Board . . . and from there to control or manipulate the nation . . . or to lose it through foolishness!

**A
Warning
Unheeded**

In 1776 the United States secured its political freedom. Congress was given the power "to coin Money, (and) regulate the Value thereof." Alexander Hamilton and

---

[1] Des Griffin, *Fourth Reich of the Rich* (California: Emissary Publications, 1978), p. 163.

Robert Morris were successful in convincing the new Congress that this phrase was not to be taken literally but only as "*implied or suggested*" powers. This enabled the Bank of North America to be founded in 1781 along the same lines as the Bank of England.

Thomas Jefferson wrote:

> There is scarcely a king
> (or would-be king)
> in a hundred
> who would not, if he could,
> follow the example of Pharaoh —
> get first all the people's money,
> then all their lands,
> and then make them and their children
> servants forever.

Are we not drifting to this position today?

In 1789 George Washington appointed Alexander Hamilton as Secretary of the Treasury. In 1790 Hamilton urged Con-

The first coin struck for the United States was in 1787. It was called the Fugio Cent and was commissioned by the Board of Treasury. Alexander Hamilton, Secretary of the Treasury, was known for his entangling alliances.

On one side of the Fugio Cent were 13 circles representing the Union. On the other side, the word "*Fugio*" means "*time flies.*" The sun emblem has pagan origins.

gress to charter a privately owned corporation as the Bank of the United States. This private bank would have the sole right of issuing currency for the United States. Jefferson strongly opposed this but George Washington signed the bill on February 25, 1791.

**A Den
Of Vipers**

General Andrew Jackson recognized the evil of this money system and in addressing bankers, said:

> You are a den of vipers.
> I intend to rout you out.

In a veto message printed to the Senate on July 10, 1832, President Jackson said, in part:

> It is neither necessary nor proper
> (for the Government)
> to transfer its legislative power
> to such a bank,
> and therefore unconstitutional.
> It is to be regretted
> that the rich and powerful
> too often bend the acts of Government
> to their selfish purposes . . .

It is interesting to note that under Jackson's leadership the National Debt was reduced to zero! This was the only time in our entire history that the United States government did not owe one cent!

Some claim it was the money barons who created the depressions of 1890 and 1907 in order to install a money system to their liking. Indeed, the supporters of the Federal Reserve Act of 1913 did promise that it would stabilize the dollar. Americans would never again see the dollar madly fluctuate nor, they said, would the dollar lose its purchasing power.

President Wilson recognized the dangers:

A great industrial nation is controlled
by its system of credit.
The growth of the nations, therefore,
and all our activities
are in the hands of
a few men.

We have come to be one of the worst
ruled,
one of the most completely
controlled governments
in the civilized world —
no longer a government of free opinion,
no longer a government by conviction
or a vote of the majority,
but a government by the opinion and
duress
of a small group of dominant men.

(National Economy and
the Banking System,
Senate Documents, Col. 3, No. 23
75th Congress, 1st Session, 1939)

**The
Warburgs**

Stephen Birmingham (in his book, *Our Crowd*, Dell Publishing Co., New York, 1967, p. 400) alleges that the person who played the most significant part in getting the Federal Reserve System adopted was Paul Warburg. He and his brother, Felix, had come to the United States from Germany in 1902. Their brother Max ran the family bank in Frankfurt, Germany.

Paul Warburg married Nina Loeb of Kuhn, Loeb and Company. There were close alliances with John D. Rockefeller, Jr. and Jacob Schiff. Rockefeller's agent admitted many years later:

> Despite my views
> about the value to society
> of greater publicity
> for the affairs of corporations,
> there was an occasion,
> near the close of 1910,
> when I was secretive,
> indeed as furtive,
> as any conspirator.
>
> I do not feel it is any exaggeration
> to speak of our secret expedition
> to Jekyl Island (off the coast of Georgia)
> as the occasion of the actual conception
> of what eventually became
> the Federal Reserve System.[1]

The Influence Of Colonel House

Surprisingly enough, although Woodrow Wilson publicly opposed the Wall Street "money trust" ... privately Wilson was influenced by none other than "Colonel" Edward Mandel House. House was a front for the "internationalists" who sought a central bank and income tax. His ultimate aim was socialism.

In the Intimate Papers of Colonel House, edited by Charles Seymour, Volume 1, page 114, President Wilson is reported to have said:

> Mr. House is my second personality.
> He is my independent self.
> His thoughts and mine are one.
> If I were in his place,
> I would do just as he suggested.

The above may possibly be falsely attri-

---

[1] Frank Vanderlip, *Farm Boy to Financier* (Pennsylvania: Saturday Evening Post, February 9, 1935), p. 25.

buted to Wilson . . . as it sounds so unlike his other words and so out of character. If it is false, it nevertheless, shows us what appeared to be the case to some observers at the time.

Charles A. Lindbergh Sr., father of the famous aviator, warned at that time:

The invisible government
by the money power . . .
will create inflation
whenever the trusts want inflation!
(Congressional Record,
December 22, 1913)

Both Teddy Roosevelt and Woodrow Wilson had the wide support of Wall Street. Wilson became President and the Federal Reserve Act was passed by Congress on December 22, 1913.

**The
Power
Of The
New York
Branch!**

The Federal Reserve System influences the flow of credit and money in the United States. All national banks, by law, are required to belong to the Federal Reserve System. The system consists of 12 "*National Banks.*" The Federal Reserve *Board*

Newspaper clippings above from 1929 Wall Street crash. Note headline on Rockefeller. We will witness a similar disaster soon paving the way for Antichrist and greater controls!

of Governors consists of 7 members appointed by the President of the United States. Each member serves 14 years. The most important Federal Reserve Bank of the 12 is the New York branch. The international bankers use the Federal Reserve as their whipping boy to achieve their power-hungry aims.

Howard J. Ruff, an economic analyst, sees in the near future:

1. Exploding inflation
2. Price controls
3. Erosion of your savings (eventually to nothing)
4. A collapse of private as well as government pension programs
5. Vastly more government regulation to control your life
6. An international monetary holocaust which will sweep all paper currency down the drain and turn the world upside down.[1]

Power In Hands Of Few!

The Federal Reserve System is just one small piece of the puzzle, as we see a free people fitting into a one-world society.

You can look for the current American currency system to collapse one of these days. It was the brilliant economist, Ludwig Von Mises, who said:

Government is the only institution
that can take a valuable commodity
like paper,
and make it worthless by applying ink.

---

[1] Howard J. Ruff, How To Prosper During The Coming Bad Years (New York: Times Books, 1979), p. 14.

Printing money has always been a governmental specialty. In fact, it's the one thing they do well. Howard J. Ruff reveals that the United States banking system is dominated by no more than 15 banking groups, most of them controlled by giant holding companies.

These banking holding companies include:

First National City Bank of New York
Chase Manhattan Bank
Chemical New York Corp.
Manufacturers Hanover Corp.
Marine Midland Banks, Inc.
Morgan Guaranty
Bank of America
Waschovia Corp.
Continental Bank of Chicago
The Mellon Bank
Security Pacific Corp.
Western Bank Corp.

Many Happy Returns, Americans.

JUNE 1980

In June your take-home pay is really yours!

© AMWAY Corp.

**Loans
Without
Repayment**

Banks can, in effect, create money out of thin air . . . just as the United States government can. You may be surprised to learn that for every $1000 you have in the bank, there is only about $12 to insure it! Yet the United States Government has made loans of over $200 Billion in foreign loans. Much of these loans will never be repaid . . . thus making the U.S. position even more fragile for *"big interest"* takeovers.

Chase Manhattan, Bank of America, First National City Bank of New York have more than half of their loans and their earnings coming from overseas. They could be considered the world's monetary system. Howard J. Ruff states that the Federal Government has a published national debt of $650 Billion but actually has some SIX TRILLION DOLLARS in liabilities.

If this is true, the federal obligation alone is 20 times more than the total money supply.

**How Much
Is
One Billion?**

When money reaches $1 Million . . . let alone $1 Billion . . . it is hard for us to relate to it. Perhaps this example will help.

A man gave his wife $1 Million.
He told her to go out
and spend $1000 a day.
She did.
Three years later she returned to tell him
that the money was all gone.
She wanted more!

He then gave her $1 BILLION.
He told her to go out
and spend $1000 a day.
She didn't come back
for 3000 years!

The Rothschilds

Internationally, another name linked with extreme wealth has been the family of the Rothschilds. In a history of the very rich, this final paragraph appears on the Rothschilds:

> In the realm of banking
> the name of Rothschild
> is still one to conjure with.
>
> One of the great ceremonies
> of the financial world
> occurs on each trading day in London
> when five men gather in the same room
> to set the opening price of gold
> on the world market.
>
> Of these five expert money managers,
> one is representative of the
> house of Rothschild,
> and the room where they meet
> is in the Rothschild Bank[1]

[1] Joseph J. Thorndike, Jr., The Very Rich (New York: American Heritage Publishing Co., 1976), p. 170.

Government policy is responsible for inflation . . . paying for deficit spending by "creating money" out of thin air. That debases the currency . . . makes every dollar worth less. That's inflation.

Inflation can be cured

. . . if our leaders admit the cause.

© AMWAY Corp.

Keeping this in mind, it has been estimated that the Rockefeller assets alone are possibly above $5 BILLION.[1]

Howard E. Kershner, a recognized authority on the workings of governments and their economic policies (and a Christian) wrote:

*Every government
that has had the privilege
of printing all the money it wanted
has destroyed its fiscal system.*

*I know of no currency in history
that has lasted more than 42 years
after its intrinsic base has been
abandoned.*

*Twenty-four years ago (in 1933)
this country left the gold standard,
and unless we return to it,
the life expectancy of our dollar
is not more than 20 years.*[2]

The dollar has lasted more than 42 years. But all signs point to a giant monetary upheaval in the near future.

**Time
Will
Tell**

It will be interesting to watch the power plays of the Internationalists. Presently the world is vibrating with chaos. When the pieces of the puzzle settle into a recognizable picture, will it reveal that the international bankers manipulated the Federal Reserve System to bring the United States to its knees financially?

Will it reveal that there was a ribbon of

---

[1] Ferdinand Lundberg, The Rich and the Super-Rich (New York: Lyle Stuart, Inc., 1968), p. 162.

[2] Howard E. Kershner, God, Gold and Government (New Jersey: Prentice-Hall, Inc., 1957), p. 70.

conspiracy that began hundreds of years ago . . . a conspiracy to a one-world government? Will it reveal that the money barons of today were involved in a plan for international control?

And from all of this . . . will is give birth to the rise of Antichrist?

We are reminded of the parable of the rich fool who decided to pull down his barns and build greater ones to store his wealth.

> But God said to him,
> Thou fool,
> this night thy soul
> shall be required of thee;
> then whose shall those things be,
> which thou hast provided?
> So is he
> that layeth up treasure for himself,
> and is not rich toward God.
>
> (Luke 12:20, 21)

The money manipulators, whomever they may be, will have to answer to God!

25

THE COUNCIL ON FOREIGN RELATIONS . . . THE POWER BEHIND THE THRONE?

**Designs
On
Power**

The Council of Foreign Relations (CFR) was formed in 1921 when it became evident that the United States was not going to join the League of Nations. Its founder was Colonel Edward House.

House was a British-eduction son of a financier who had British financial interests in the United States. House became President Wilson's right-hand man and emerged as virtually *"President-in-control."* House had two pet projects he wanted rammed through.

1. A Central Banking System
2. Graduated Income Tax

**House
And
His
Influence**

He was successful in seeing that both were adopted into law. It was House who brought into being the Federal Reserve Act, which benefited international bankers. The original Federal Reserve Board was largely hand-picked by "Colonel" House. House was an admirer of Karl Marx.

Edward M. House (left) was President Wilson's closest friend and trusted advisor. House was a front for the "internationalists" who sought a central bank and income tax. His ultimate aim was socialism.

President Wilson sought to push through the League of Nations treaty. In effect, it would have surrendered national sovereignty. Today, once more, there is a combined effort among the money manipulators to achieve this same end. Could this be the End Time conspiracy that ushers in Antichrist?

Those hand selected men brought in to help House included: Walter Lippman, John Foster Dulles, Allen Dulles and Christian Herter.

Two years before the United States entered the war in World War 2 (in 1939), a committee on Post-War Problems was initiated at the suggestion of the Council on Foreign Relations (CFR). Yet the CFR claims to be a "private organization that does not formulate any policy of the Government."

When the United Nations Conference met in San Francisco in 1945, there were 74 CFR members in the U.S. delegation! These included Alger Hiss, Harry Dexter White, Owen Lattimore, Nelson Rockefeller, John Foster Dulles and Dean Acheson.

It was Colonel House who authored the anonymous book, *Philip Dru—Administrator*. (He later admitted writing it.) In this book House outlined detailed plans for the creation of a One-World totalitarian government.

A Strange Resemblance

A close study of the foreign policy recommendations of the Communist Party in the United States with the foreign policy recommendations of the Council on Foreign Relations shows a strange resemblance. This is due to the fact that all types of utopian (heavenly) societies . . . Satanic, communistic and naive do-gooders, . . . all claim to have ultimate world peace and world order as their final goal.

Ultimate Goals

In Study No. 7, published by the Council on Foreign Relations on November 25,

1959 and in further statements by CFR members the following is recommended:

1. **GENERAL**
   (a) *Build a new international order (which) must be responsive to world aspirations for peace, (and) for social and economic change . . . an international order . . . including states (nations) labeling themselves as "Socialist."*
   (b) *Our broader and ultimate objective . . . is a universal community of nations.*

2. **UNITED NATIONS**
   Maintain and gradually increase the authority of the UN.

Much more is involved including a recommendation of secret negotiations with Russia on disarmament, increased foreign aid with no strings attached and recognition of Red China. All this has now come to pass!

The Rockefeller Money

The Council on Foreign Relations struggled along until 1927. It was at that time that Rockefeller money started to pour in. Then the Carnegie Foundation and the Ford Foundation started to finance the Council.

Some believe that the CFR is a *"front"* for the intellectual leaders and the international bankers who hope to control the world through the Fabian technique of sophisticated *"gradualism."*

The CFR is a secret organization. In its 1966 Annual Report, Members who do not adhere to secrecy can be dropped from membership.

An Intellectual Dictatorship

Rear Admiral Chester Ward was a member of the CFR for 16 years. He became aware that this organization was an *"intellectual dictatorship."* In an exposé of the CFR, in his book, *"Kissinger On The Couch,"* he wrote:

> *Previous attempts to document the CFR's influence have been ignored or smeared by the Liberal press as "exaggerated." This is to be expected, considering the beachheads that Key CFR members hold in all parts of the media, and especially because any attempt to tell the truth about the power and activities of CFR members is bound to be exaggerated.*
>
> *Actually, however, all the published accounts thus far have understated the CFR's influence, just as all previous accounts of Henry Kissinger's power vastly underestimate him (Page 148).*

Allen W. Dulles, who was President of the CFR also, subsequently, was appointed head of the C.I.A. (Central Intelligence Agency). And the Ford Foundation alone has given over $1 Million dollars to the CFR!

The Invisible Government

The CFR has been called *"the invisible government,"* and *"the Establishment."* It is interesting to note that members of the CFR have at one time or another staffed almost every key position of every administration since that of Franklin Delano Roosevelt! Yet most Americans have never heard of the Council on Foreign Relations! It has been successful in maintaining its semi-anonymity for over 50 years!

**Power
Seekers**

CFR members are allegedly included among the most influential international banking organizations. Major corporations have influential CFR members as do the major communications media!

God alone is the discerner of our hearts. It is not our intent in this book to smear any organization, company or individual nor to assume "guilt by association." Many people belong to organizations whose ways are evil but the individuals themselves may honestly be unaware of their evil purposes. Each individual will be judged by God who can cut through our innermost thoughts and expose us for what we really are. He knows about everyone, everywhere. Nothing can be hidden from Him.

*For the Word of God
is quick and powerful,
and sharper than any
two-edged sword,
piercing even to the
dividing asunder
of soul and spirit,
and of the joints and marrow,
and is a discerner of the thoughts
and intents of the heart!*

(Hebrews 4:12)

God also warns us that:

*He that rejecteth Me,
and receiveth not My Words,
hath One that judgeth him:
the Word that I have spoken,
the same shall judge him in the last day.*

(John 12:48)

**Foreign
Affairs**

The CFR issues a quarterly magazine, *Foreign Affairs*. Its Editorial Advisory Board has included Henry Kissinger. William P. Bundy has been its Editor.

The Bible tells us: *"Ye shall know them by their fruits"* (Matthew 7:16). Let's look at one of the most important policy articles published by CFR's *Foreign Affairs* magazine. Take the time to read it very carefully. Remember, CFR is an organization of intellectuals. Their approach to a One World solution is very subtle. We can recognize communism as a threat but few people recognize the other hidden threat of the intellectual "gradualism" approach!

A 14-page article appeared in the January, 1973 issue of *Foreign Affairs* (An American Quarterly Review), pages 286-299. The article is titled, *The Changing Essence of Power* by Seyom Brown.

Seyom Brown, Senior Fellow at the Brookings Institute, Washington; is the author of *"The Faces of Power: Constancy and Change in United States Foreign Policy from Truman to Johnson."*

**Towards
One World**

The article is quoted here only in part. We printed some of the direct quotes in boldface although boldface type does not appear in original article.

> Today's political flux features on its diplomatic surface three interacting trends: a disintegration of the cold-war coalitions, the rise of nonsecurity issues to the top of diplomatic agendas, and a diversification of friendships and adversary relations.
>
> These surface movements are the expres-

sion of deeper currents, **which if appropriately exploited by providential statesmanship, could fundamentally alter the essence of world politics, changing the structures and ingredients of power itself . . . .**

If the dominant tendencies continue to mature as indicated above, an international system whose essential characteristics are grossly different not only from the bipolar cold-war system (U.S. and Russia) but also from previous "balance of power" systems **(this international system) could emerge full blown, very likely by the 1980s . . . .**

What, then, becomes of today's great powers, especially the two superpowers? How would they stand under new criteria of power? . . . The nine or more members of the European Economic Community (Common Market countries), when acting as a unit on particular international issues, could well emerge **as an equally powerful unit in world politics.** *(Author's note: Now can you see how the United States of EUROPE will become supremely powerful with Antichrist as its head!) . . . .*

What then are the requirements of a providential statesmanship that will increase the likelihood of the world's political development toward a more peaceful and just world order? . . .

Here we paraphrase for brevity.

1. The United States and Russia must not utilize their military superiority as a bargaining advantage.

2. The wealthiest countries (U.S. etc.) must stop attempting to maintain "spheres of dominance, or even to maintain permanent extended alliance systems."

3. The United States and other leading nations should actively cooperate with countries in "*rival ideological blocs.*"

4. A world system should correct any imbalances through a world political economy.

5. "*New sets of representative institutions will need to be elaborated and empowered on regional and global bases to ensure that all communities affected have a fair say over how these common goods (from the ocean, the atmosphere and outer space) are used.*" [**Paraphrasing ends here.**]

The article continues:

> Is the United States likely to be one of those societies that constructively comes to grips with the new forces? . . .
>
> There appears to be growing support for policies that would reduce the foreign commitments of the United States, bring the American military personnel home, trim the defense budget and cut foreign military and economic assistance . . .

Reshaping Foreign Policy

The article ends by recommending that U.S. foreign policy be reshaped along 5 definite lines (remember, this was written in 1973!):

1. *The United States, by its own example, would **play down** the use of force as a sanction behind diplomacy . . .*

2. *The United States would seek out special opportunities for practical **cooperative projects** with those with whom it has general ideological disagreements.*

3. *The United States would cooperate in funneling substantial capital and other resources from the rich to the poor*

countries through **international** institutions . . . It will be necessary to develop **new world community** and world
interest rationals as motivating ap-
peals.

4. The United States would make it at-
tractive to others to share in the opportunities now arising to develop **global
systems** for exploiting the earth's
wealth for the benefit of mankind.

5. Finally, (in giving **money** to other
countries) . . . the recipient countries
would be given more responsibility . . .
for the allocations and setting the conditions of repayment . . .

In short, the people of the United States
in the first instance would have to be
more forthcoming than they have been
in dispensing with some of the traditional trappings of national sovereignty. (Author's note: This is a typical
intellectual "gradualism" approach to a
One World Government).

A foreign policy responsive to these
guidelines would be consistent with the
basic international objectives of the
United States since the end of the Second World War . . .

It does mean that we must free ourselves
from the snares of inertia and false
pride so as not to confuse the policies
and commitments of the past with the
fundamental objectives they were supposed to serve.

**Destroying
Patriotism**

Now, if you have read this rather long ex-
cerpt very carefully, you will see how
sinister and subtle is the "intellectual
dictatorship" in its striving to accomplish
its One World aims. In the last paragraph

they equate *"false pride"* with old fashioned patriotism.

And this is very important! Note how they state in the second to the last paragraph quoted that, in effect, these 5 points of *"enlightened"* foreign policy are consistent with the basic foreign policy the United States government has been following since World War 2!

A Strange Coincidence

What they do not realize in printing this is that this is a direct admission of guilt on their part, revealing the influence and power of the CFR. The CFR states that it does not formulate any policy of the Government. And, on the surface, this may be true. But what it does is make sure that CFR members are in high, influential positions in the U.S. Government. It is precisely these officials, who are CFR members, who have the ability, if they so choose, to make sure U.S. policy is along CFR One World lines.

And by their fruits we are beginning to recognize this web of naïve surrender to one world government.

Oh, what a tangled web we weave
When first we practice to deceive!

God's Word tells us: " . . . *be sure your sin will find you out"* (Numbers 32:23).

The CFR had influence during the administrations of FDR, Truman, Eisenhower, Kennedy, Johnson, Nixon and Carter. Nixon did, however, sever connections with the CFR. Did this perhaps have any-

The Watergate Affair

thing to do with his sudden resignation from the Presidency?

The Watergate affair was blown way out of proportion by both the Washington Post and The New York Times as well as major television networks. The news of high political officials attempting to quiet publicity over a thirdrate burglary hardly rates continuous front page coverage and prime time television exposure. Could this troublesome issue have been fanned hotter as part of a well-orchestrated plot to aid in eliminating a non-cooperating President who fell from the graces of the CFR and its allies? No one can answer that for sure!

On February 4, 1945, Prime Minister Winston Churchill, President Franklin D. Roosevelt and Premier Joseph Stalin met at a famous Black Sea resort near Yalta. Stalin won a victory by having Germany and Berlin divided. Such an agreement assured continued world turmoil for the future! Was this a carefully engineered plot by the internationalists for One World?

But we do know that CFR-type policies flourished during wars engaged in by the United States.

The Yalta Give-away

In World War 2, Franklin D. Roosevelt met with Churchill and Stalin in February, 1945 at <u>Yalta</u>. The Allies were close to victory. Yalta is the Crimean summer resort on the Black Sea.

The Big Three agreed on plans to create an organization called the United Nations. Roosevelt made many concessions at Yalta giving Russia control of Eastern Europe and part of Germany. In July, 1945, freedom's death was further sealed by Harry S. Truman who met with British Prime Minister Clement Attlee and Stalin. German East Prussia was turned over to Russia. Millions of Germans were forced into areas of Germany now controlled by Russia.

The Korea Give-away

In the <u>Korean War,</u> a CFR member, Owen Lattimore, revealed the strategy (according to Dr. Carroll Quigley) . . . South Korea was to fall, but it was not to look as though we pushed her.[1] What happened is history. General Douglas MacArthur had defeated the North Korean army and sought to finalize the war by destroying the several hundred thousand Chinese who had swept down from China. President Harry Truman relieved MacArthur of his command. Again the CFR saw a strategic battle towards its One-World policies won.

---

[1] W. Cleon Skousen, *The Naked Capitalist*, (Salt Lake City, Utah: Skousen Publishing, 1970), p. 78.

**The
Vietnam
Give-away**

When it became evident that Barry Gold-water might possibly win the Presidency . . . the liberal progressive forces combined their powers to make sure Lyndon Johnson was elected. They tried to force Johnson, during the Vietnam War, to follow a course of *"peace at any price."* When Johnson balked, he was politically ripped to shreds. He became a one-term President. We lost the war in Vietnam and the communists scored another victory!

Observe the scene today. The United States has adopted a *"no-win"* appeasement policy towards hostile nations. Russia maintains forces at our own back door, Cuba, and the U.S. stands idly by. Watch as this *"anti-nationalism"* policy blooms into an international One World conglom-erate known as The United States of Europe.

Yes, the Fabian Society and its Round Table of intellectuals has come a long way since 1884. It gave birth to the CFR, the Trilateralists and the Bilderbergers.

Will it reach its goal of a united world power in the 1980's? Only time will tell!

26

BILDERBERGERS ... THE POWER SEEKERS?

**Positions
Of
Power**

The CFR, the Bilderbergers, the Trilateralists all have one thing in common . . . they are secret societies. Members include the elite from the worlds of business, banking, government and the intellectual. Influential world leaders are, in many cases, members of all 3 of their international organizations.

For some time it was difficult to get any information on the Bilderbergers, their cloak of secrecy was so effective. The Justice Department and prominent Senators claimed ignorance of any existence of a group called the Bilderbergers.

But the Bilderbergers do exist! The Bilderbergers are interlocked with the CFR, the English-speaking Union, the Pilgrims Society and the Round Table. They have a heavy cross-membership in the Trilateral Commission.

**The
Inner
Circle**

While membership in the CFR averages about 1500, the Bilderbergers limit their inner circle to about 100. These elite, hand-picked 100 are invited to an annual meeting held by this international master planning conclave.

These strategy conferences are always held in secret. They have been always directed by the same chairman, Prince Bernhard of the Netherlands. The first secret meeting took place at the Bilderberg Hotel in Oosterbeek, Holland from May 29-31, 1954. The power group got its name from the Bilderberg Hotel.

**The
Rule Of
Secrecy**

Despite the imposing names of the 100 attendees, the New York Times, the Washington Post and the Minneapolis Tribune have managed not to cover this event held annually. The Bilderbergers code of secrecy has been quite successful. They have been officially referred to as The Bilderberger Group.

In 1957 the Bilderbergers met off the coast of Georgia on St. Simon's Island. In 1964 they met at Williamsburg, Virginia. Other annual meetings have been held in Canada, Turkey, Germany, England, France and Austria. Each meeting is closed to the public and to reporters. No copies of their resolutions are given to the press.

Dr. Joseph H. Retinger is credited with getting the Bilderberg movement underway. He was Communist Poland's Charge d'Affaires in Russia in 1954. Prince Bernhard was the royal consort of Queen

Juliana. She has been reported to be the richest woman in the world. Juliana and Lord Rothschild are business partners in the Shell Oil Company.

Strange Alignments

While Retinger is given the credit for starting this elite organization, others allege that Lord Rothschild and Laurance Rockefeller have played important behind-the-scenes parts in this world drama. It is interesting to note that this secret Bilderberg group has held meetings in the small, remote town of Woodstock, Vermont in the Woodstock Inn. What makes this interesting is the Woodstock Inn is owned by Laurance Rockefeller!

In Europe, the Rothschilds have hosted meetings. The 1962 and 1973 meetings were hosted by the Wallenbergs. The Wallenbergs reportedly have a fortune estimated at $10 Billion!

Among those who have attended these secret meetings are: David and Nelson Rockefeller, Robert McNamara, Henry Kissinger, Gerald Ford, Margaret Thatcher, President Valery Giscard D'Estang of France, Harold Wilson, Edward Heath (both Wilson and Heath were heads of two political parties in Britain), McGeorge Bundy (who became President of the Ford Foundation).

Other well-known attendees include: J. William Fulbright (former U.S. Senator), Jacob Javits (Republican Senator from New York), H.J. Heinz II (President of the H.J. Heinz Company), George W. Ball, General

Walter Bedell Smith and General Andrew J. Goodpaster who was Supreme Allied Commander in Europe. Goodpaster later became Superintendent of West Point Academy. The type of hazing tolerated under Goodpaster's leadership included the forcing of men and women cadets to kill chickens by biting their necks with their teeth. In one hazing incident cadets dressed in Ku Klux Klan garb. Outside pressures brought these incidents to an end. Men from Look, Time and The Washington Post have also attended but none chose to write on the subject.

When a reporter asked Gerald R. Ford why the two meetings he attended were secret, he replied:

> I'm also a 33rd degree Mason
> and a member of Delta Kappa Epsilon,
> Phi Delta Phi and Michigamus . . .
> all secret societies.

Well Guarded

Secrecy is one characteristic of the Bilderbergers. When they hold their meetings as many as 1000 troops surround their meeting place. Their meetings generally last 3 days.

The American Friends of Bilderbergers, with offices in New York City, is an IRS-approved charitable establishment. It has been alleged that Exxon, Atlantic Richfield and IBM have been regular contributors. The papers of incorporation of the New York organization include George W. Ball and Henry J. Heinz. Ball was a Foreign Policy consultant to President Nixon and also a member of the CFR.

In the April 20-23, 1978 meeting at Princeton, David Rockefeller, Henry Kissinger and Giovanni Angelli arrived in bulletproof limousines, surrounded by escort vehicles of bodyguards with submachine guns. Giovanni Angelli is chairman of Fiat, an Italian automobile company. Also present were Zbigniew Brzezinski (Assistant to President Carter for National Security Affairs) and General Alexander Haig, former Kissinger assistant and European NATO Force Commander.

Death Of Dollar

In this April 1978 meeting the European Bilderbergers predicted a depression would strike the world in 1979 and that the U.S. dollar would die. **The solution, Bilderberger leaders said was the dumping of the dollar for an international "bancor" system.**

The planning at the secret Princeton meeting revolved around the creation of a new currency that would take the dollar's place in the world market . . . a currency that would be universally acceptable as a medium of exchange. David Rockefeller, whose Chase Manhattan Bank, has led the world in currency speculation, perhaps now saw the handwriting on the wall. Rockefeller's power was diminishing . . . the dollar would nosedive. We would enter an era of inflationary depression.

The words *"inflationary depression"* sound contradictory . . . but they are not. Most people think of a Depression as a time when people are selling apples and there is a scarcity of money.

An <u>Inflationary Depression</u> is the same illness . . . but at a much more critical stage! In an Inflationary Depression . . . there is plenty of money, but its purchasing power is severely curtailed! Ten dollars may buy you 2 apples!

A New Leader

In the 1980 meeting of the Bilderbergers, the Bilderberg Group met still again under the guidance of an international steering committee. This was the 28th meeting since Bilderberg's inception in 1954. At the 1980 meeting, held in Germany, Lord Alex-Douglas Home (former British prime minister) stepped down. Former West German President Walter Scheel, 60, replaced the aging Lord Alex-Douglas Home. The old guard has given way to younger leaders in an important reorganization plan.

The person scheduled to take William P. Bundy's place as Bilderberg honorary secretary-general for the U.S. is Paul B. Finney, executive editor of *Fortune* magazine. It is interesting to note that William P. Bundy has been editor of *Foreign Affairs*, the official voice of the Council on Foreign Relations (CFR).

The question many ask is are officials of the Government, who are members of the CFR and the Bilderberg organization compromising their position by aligning with those who seek a One World government? Does it not weaken the position of national sovereignty of the United States and prepare the way for Antichrist, a satanic world ruler?

If it does not . . . why the secrecy? If it does not . . . why restricted membership to those only who are the manipulators of power through vast control of money, through the mass media and through politics?

Is there a conspiracy? Are the Bilderbergers part of it? Or are they merely another group of would be do-gooders used and manipulated by other unseen forces? World events are shaping up so rapidly in these End Times that the answer to that question may not be far off . . . maybe within a few years . . . or months!

27

THE TRILATERAL COMMISSION ... AMERICA'S NEW SECRET GOVERNMENT

**One
World
Goal**

The Trilateral Commission is an extension of the Council on Foreign Relations (CFR). Its ultimate goal is to incorporate Japan, Canada, the United States and the Common Market nations of Europe into a one-world socialistic governmental web.

The name, TRILATERAL, is derived from the fact that the leaders come from three democratic areas of the world ... the United States, Western Europe and Japan.

It was David Rockefeller who hand-picked this elite group of some 250 individuals in 1973 to begin this organization. They included power shapers from business, banking, government, labor and the intelligencia.

On the surface this group would appear to be accomplishing good, seeking ways to make a positive contribution to world problems. The Trilateral Commission meets twice a year to discuss problems like the world monetary situation, economic issues and military issues. However, those who have penetrated the inner workings of this group state that the real purpose is to take over all key policy-making positions in government and to unite the free world into a loosely knitted socialistic world government.[1]

In order to overhaul the present international system, the Trilateralists have a long range plan which includes:

1. Formation of a joint policymaking institution among Trilateral countries to coordinate economic and political relations with the Third World and Communist-bloc nations.

2. A policy for keeping peace which involves decreasing military forces and nuclear capabilities . . . to seek at all cost to avert confrontation, even if it means knuckling under enemy threats at the expense of abandoning our allies. The United States has already done this by turning our backs on Free China (Taiwan), and by allowing Russia to maintain military bases in Cuba.

3. A restructuring of three international economic institutions:
    A. The International Monetary Fund (IMF)
    B. The General Agreement on Tariffs and Trade (GATT)
    C. The World Bank

International Monetary Fund

The International Monetary Fund was begun after World War 2. It was designed to help nations adjust to free trade by providing financial assistance. However, the new International Monetary Fund (func-

---

[1] W.S. McBirnie, *The Trilateral Commission* (Glendale, California: C.C.A.), p. 3.

tioning like the Federal Reserve System) would be able to create money and also to restrict the creation of money.

This would be done by the issuing of a new currency called Bancor (sometimes called SDR or Special Drawing Rights). This new money would replace gold and the dollar as the world monetary unit. All currencies would be tied into Bancor . . . even your traveler's checks! This international money system would mean that those in charge of it would have absolute world power. For in this world, money means power.

Which do men strive for the most . . . money or power? Have you ever noticed men of extreme wealth who simply were not happy or satisfied? What do they do? They run for public office. They are willing to spend a large portion of their accumulated fortunes. They are willing to run day and night, politicking, shaking hands, making speeches. Why? Because money does not fill the void. They seek POWER!

It was Lord Acton who said in 1887:

> Power tends to corrupt;
> absolute power corrupts absolutely.

In essence, the CFR, the Bilderbergers, the Trilateralists seek power. That power will corrupt and someday usher in the age of Antichrist.

An Interesting History

It is interesting to observe that most every aspect of Jimmy Carter's foreign policy in the late 1970's reflected a Trilateralist viewpoint. His program of foreign policy became an appeasement of Cuba, Panama, Red China and Russia. His withdrawal of major troops from South Korea is part of the Trilateralist Plan.

Jeremiah Novak, who has had articles published in the *Christian Science Monitor* is reported to have said in a radio interview with Ray Briem on February 19, 1977 (in describing a Trilateral document, written by Richard Cooper):

> Page 21 says the public and leaders of most countries continue to live in a mental universe which no longer exists, a world of separate nations and that have great difficulty thinking in terms of global perspectives and interdependence . . .
>
> What he is saying is we no longer live in a world of sovereign nations — and that applies to the United States as well. We just celebrated last year our Bicentennial of independence. In November of this year (1976), in this document, we have issued a new declaration of interdependence which will greatly modify the sovereignty of this country.

(Mr. Novak, himself, is not a Trilateralist.)

Towards Socialized Government

In the past few years we have seen the continued gradual approach to centralized government control of our lives through socialistic programs. These include recent energy programs, socializing and welfare programs, guaranteed annual wage, social security and medical security programs. On the surface they may appear beneficial, but they all eventually will lead to a people who become subservient (submissive) to Big Brother.

WITHDRAWAL
LIMIT
TODAY

$25

FIRST NATIONAL BANK

One day you will drive up to your bank and discover a limit placed on the amount of money you can withdraw! With financial institutions having only about 5% in liquid cash . . . a run on banks would be disastrous. Withdrawals could be prohibited!

Perhaps you did not realize that the U.S. Government can freeze your bank account! The President now has the power to announce the existence of a national emergency via **Executive Order #11921** (June 15, 1976), **#11490** (October 30, 1969) and other Executive Orders. These orders have behind them the force of the law which could be used to establish a federal dictatorship.

Under these orders federal agencies can:

1. Control all food supply
2. Control all money and credit
3. Control all transportation
4. Control all communication
5. Control all public utilities

All this can come into being by the President merely signing a piece of paper that a *"national emergency exists."*

Emergency Banking Regulations

Under the Emergency Banking Regulation No. 1, if this were to occur:

1. Your bank accounts would be immediately frozen, both checking and savings.
2. You could be prohibited from making any withdrawals of cash.
3. You could be prohibited from writing any more checks without the bank's approval, except for *"customary"* amounts. The bank would decide what is *"customary."*
4. No checks would be honored by any bank for any *"unauthorized purpose."*

Such actions, in effect, could allow a President so inclined to surrender the sovereignty of the United States and mold it into a one-world, socialistic pattern.

But there's more. Similar laws also allow the President to:

1. Control or prohibit all CB radio transmission;
2. Confiscate "excess and surplus real and personal property" owned by private citizens;
3. Ration virtually the entire output of American industry;
4. Shut down every private school in the country and take possession of the buildings for government use.

There are hundreds of regulations included in this Emergency Powers plan which include seizing property, instituting of martial law, controlling travel . . . all which in effect control the lives of American citizens.

Powerful Central Government

What we are witnessing on a gradual level is the restructuring of the United States into a powerful Federally-controlled nation. Many believe that the Trilateral Commission's immediate wish is the domination of the United States through the Executive Branch. The Trilateral Commission is not merely a passive discussion group but an active influential one. It has been successful in helping to control the Executive Branch of the U.S. Government to move in its desired direction.

Aiding in the founding of the Trilateral Commission was Zbigniew Brzezinski. Under the Carter administration,

Brzezinski was Assistant to the President for National Security. The Trilateralists were able to place one third of their members into top level Administration positions during Jimmy Carter's presidency.

In his book, *Between Two Ages*, Brzezinski wrote:

> The approaching two-hundredth anniversary of the Declaration of Independence could justify the call for a national constitutional convention to re-examine the nation's formal institutional framework.
>
> Either 1976 or 1989 — the two-hundredth anniversary of the Constitution — could serve as a suitable target date culminating a national dialogue on the relevance of existing arrangements . . . Realism, however, forces us to recognize that the necessary political innovation will not come from direct constitutional reform, desirable as that would be. The needed change is more likely to develop incrementally and less overtly . . . in keeping with the American tradition of blurring distinctions between public and private institutions.[1]

Brzezinski also wrote in this book that mankind has moved through three great stages of evolution . . . and is in the middle of the fourth and final stage.

Four Stage Plan

The **first stage** was religious, combining a heavenly *"universalism provided by the acceptance of the idea that man's destiny is essentially in God's hands"* with an earthly *"narrowness derived from massive*

---

[1] Zbigniew Brzezinski, *Between Two Ages* (New York: The Viking Press, 1970), pp. 258, 259, 260.

ignorance, illiteracy, and a vision confined to the immediate environment."

The **second stage** was nationalism, matching Christian equality with national equality before the law, which "marked another giant step in the progressive redefinition of man's nature and place in our world."

The **third stage** was Marxism, which, says Brzezinski, "represents a further vital and creative stage in the maturing of man's universal vision." This appears on page 72 of Between Two Ages.

The fourth and **final stage** is what Brzezinski calls the "Technetronic Era." This is the result of American-Communist evolutionary transformations or the ideal of rational humanism on a global scale.

This is the type of philosophy which dominates the Trilateral Commission and which dominates the Executive Branch of the United States government.

Strange Coincidence

Many have asked if it is mere coincidence that an obscure peanut farmer was named a member of the Trilateral Commission as soon as it was founded. Was it a coincidence that this peanut farmer, Jimmy Carter, was groomed by Zbigniew Brzezinski, supported by the Rockefeller's and Time magazine to become President. Then when Carter became President, was it a coincidence that all the Trilateralists and Rockefeller Foundation and Coca-Cola people were chosen by Carter simply because of their ability?

Trilateral Members who were in the Carter Administration included:

1. Zbigniew Brzezinski,
   National Security Advisor
2. Cyrus Vance, Secretary of State
3. Walter Mondale, Vice President
4. Harold Brown, Secretary of Defense
5. Andrew Young,
   U.S. Ambassador to the United Nations

Executives of many of the major banking institutions are Trilateralists. One writer in commenting of the power of the Trilateral Commission claimed in part:

> The presidency of the United States and the key cabinet departments of the federal government have been taken over by a private organization dedicated to the subordination of the domestic interests of the United States to the international interests of the multi-national banks and corporations.
>
> It would be unfair to say that the Trilateral Commission dominates the Carter Administration. The Trilateral Commission is the Carter Administration.
>
> Craig S. Karpel
> Cartergate: The Death of Democracy

Six Questions

Is Jimmy Carter a born again Christian? We are not to be the judge of this. As Christians, we must exercise grace and love with wisdom. Some things we would question:

1. His seemingly total support of Trilateralist advisors.
2. His support of the Equal Rights Amendment.

3. His questionable fellow travelers in the field of politics and music.

4. His remarks in the interview to *Playboy Magazine*, as well as the interview itself.

5. His soft stand against anti-Christian Communism!

6. His appointment of an outspoken Protestant activist and liberal, William Sloane Coffin, to act as "Protestant Visiting Clergyman" to our Iranian hostages in December 1979.

It will be interesting to see how the Trilateralists, the CFR and the Bildebergers subtly exercise their power in the election of a President in the decision years of 1980 and 1984. Since 1840, every President elected on a "0" year in this country has died in office.

Creating Crisis Conditions

One of the Trilateralists favorite stepping-stones is during "*crisis*" conditions. Such "*crisis*" conditions allow for more Executive Branch control and contribute to unification of the U.S. with Japan and European nations. These crises include:

1. The Energy Problem . . . or Hoax

We have sufficient forms of energy resources to last us over 2000 years. Approximate supply listed below.

Natural Gas	200 years available
Petroleum	130 years available
Oil from shale	1500 years available
Coal	6000 years available

Who controls the energy resources? The oil and gas world is dominated by seven major firms. Six of these firms have Trilateral representation! They include Arco,

Exxon, Mobil, Standard Oil (Standard Oil of California and Indiana) and Texas Utilities. The Rockefeller family has personal holdings in Exxon and Standard Oil.

The major power and utility companies also have Trilateral connected bank control.

Observe how quickly the price of fuel escalated within one year, 1979 . . . from about 75¢ a gallon to over $1! Did energy suddenly become this scarce? Or is this part of a subtle plan to defuse U.S. nationalism and prepare the way for a one-world socialistic goal? Time will tell!

2. The Financial Crisis

What we are presently witnessing is the orchestration of a financial panic that will bring America to its knees and usher in greater government control. This, in part, will bring the goals of the CFR and Trilateralists a little closer.

Here is how the financial panic ingredients are put together:

First, in order to attempt to balance federal budget deficits, taxes are raised!

Second, create more dollars and so reduce the value of all existing dollars. What you may not realize is that for every $1000 you have in the bank . . . there is only $12 to insure it! In 1975 over 40% of the FDIC (bank insurance) total fund was used in just one bank failure!

Third, allow state and city governments to accumulate mountains of debt. New York City is on the verge of bankruptcy. About

70 banks hold more than 50% of their capital in New York securities!

Fourth, the United States Treasury owes more than $90 billion in overseas debts.

Fifth, the gold supply in the United States is slowly diminishing. This means the U.S. will eventually (very shortly) have to rely simply on fiat money.

What is fiat money? Fiat money is paper currency made legal tender by law, although not backed by gold or silver and not necessarily redeemable in coin.

What will this mean? It will mean that the United States will have to either

1. allow the present U.S. dollar continually to depreciate in value or
2. replace the fiat dollar with a gold backed dollar at a ratio of 10 for 1 or 10,000 for 1.

The New Dollar

A duplicate dollar currency is already printed. It is stored away at the Culpepper, Virginia facility of the Federal Reserve and at Mt. Weather in Virginia. Carl Mintz, on the staff of the House Banking Committee, is reported to have remarked: *"I believe it's (the new money) in the billions of dollars, and it's buried in lots of places."*

The Trilateralist group has been described as *"a rich man's club"* and it is. How this power will be used in the 1980's will determine whether the allegations made by concerned individuals are true or false. As Lord Acton said, *"Power tends to corrupt."* If their power becomes absolute that power will corrupt absolutely. Enter then, the age of Antichrist!

28

THE COMMON MARKET AND THE
TRILATERAL COMMISSION

**Universal
Government**

Many of the goals of the Trilateralists are being fulfilled through the Common Market of Europe.

It is possible that in our lifetime we will see much progress towards a universal government system and a new world financial order that will control all buying and selling.

It is possible that Antichrist is living today . . . waiting for conditions to be ripe for his entrance into the world scene. Antichrist will rule over the revived Roman Empire . . . Western, and possibly part of Eastern, Europe.

The Common Market is now comprised of 10 nations. Rome first appeared as a world power in 242 BC in the conquest of Sicily. For the next 300 years Rome's influence moved southward to Israel and Egypt;

You are looking at the Common Market Headquarters in Brussels, Belgium. Antichrist, quite possibly, could become the head of this union of 10 nations. Turn this page. You will note this building is shaped in the form of a stylized cross!

eastward to conquer most of the Grecian empire, westward to Spain and northward to England. Gradually this empire broke up and Italy was overrun by Barbarians in 410 AD, it fell in 476 AD, and it was finally overrun by the Germans in 963 AD.

Although the Roman empire was broken, as prophesied by Daniel chapter 2, the empire would continue to rule until the time of the end. The major wars from 1000 AD to the present time have been wars involving Roman empire nations.

Dr. David Webber, editor of *Gospel Truth*, observes:

> In 1957, six nations joined together in a trade agreement called the European Economic Community, or the Common Market. When the headquarters for the Common Market were erected in Brussels, Belgium, ten flagpoles for the flags of ten nations were erected in front of the building. This was in accordance with Bible prophecy.

Six Charter Members

The six charter members were: Belgium, France, The Netherlands, Italy, West Germany and Luxembourg. In 1973 Henry Kissinger urged Common Market members to appoint 4 more member nations. Norway, England, Denmark and Ireland were proposed for membership. Norway, however, backed out. It was not until 1979 when a tenth nation was accepted . . . Greece!

The Bible tells us that in the last days, an alliance of 10 nations, from out of what was once the Roman Empire, will control the economic and political life of the world. These 10 nations (referred to in Daniel 7:24; Revelation 17:12) could become known as the United States of EUROPE. It is possible that one of these 10 nations may drop out of the Common Market . . . thus making it possible for the United States to become eventually the final 10th nation! This is my personal belief.

It is my belief that the Common Market alliance is the alliance described in Daniel 11:23 in which Antichrist takes control. It reads:

> . . . after an alliance
> is made with him (Antichrist)
> he will practice deception,
> he will go up and gain power
> with a small force of people.

Similarities Compared

What similarities are found in the CFR, the Bilderbergers, and the Trilateral Commission?

1. They strive for secrecy.
   Secrecy can be a form of deception.
2. They strive for power.
   Because they control the world's money market, they have the ability to achieve world power.
3. They are a small force of people.
   The CFR - about 1500 members.
   The Bilderbergers - about 100 members.
   The Trilateral Commission -
   about 250 members.

Yet it is possible for this combined group of some 1850 people to control the lives of over 3 Billion people!

**The
Russian
Common
Market**

Some people believe the Common Market nations are not a power of any significance. The Russians believe otherwise. When the Common Market nations united, they recognized the threat to them of a superpower. At that time, they drew their own satellites together into a Warsaw Treaty Organization in 1955, emulating the European economic community.

The combined assets of the Common Market nations far outstrip those of the United States in almost every category. And most of those who are in control of the major portion of these assets belong to either one or a combination of the three secret organizations previously mentioned.

**Time
Will
Reveal
Truth**

It is easy to see that the Trilateral Commission certainly has a vital interest in the European community and particularly the Common Market nations.

We cannot prove conclusively whether this vital interest has also developed into a vital role with evil intent. Time alone will reveal this. The Bible does reveal the tragic role that Common Market nations will play in the end times.

Are we seeing the stage being set for this final act just prior to Armageddon? (Revelation 16:16)

For more detailed information on what will occur in the end times, you will want to read **THE RISE OF ANTICHRIST** by Salem Kirban ($4.95). Salem Kirban, Inc., 604 Mason's Mill Park, Huntingdon Valley, Penna. 19006. Add $1 to cover postage and packing.

29

SATAN'S PROGRAM FOR THE CHURCH

Satan Dedicated To His Cause

It may surprise you to know that Satan has a very active program for the Church of Jesus Christ—and in many areas he has been very successful. Why? Because he is dedicated to his cause. And so are his angels! They take no vacations, no holidays . . . not even any coffee breaks. Whenever the slightest opportunity opens up for them to send in their wrecking crew, they volunteer without any hesitation!

While at Montrose Bible Conference in the summer of 1979, I heard a challenging sermon on Satan's peril to the Church given by Rev. John Emmans, Pastor of The Church of the Open Door at Fort Washington, Pennsylvania. I am indebted to him for the outline of this chapter.

In the Seven Churches in Asia (Revelation 2 and 3), we have both every kind of church and every kind of member, which not only existed on earth in John's generation but also will exist throughout all church history.

The seven cities where the seven churches were located formed approximately a circle 100 miles in diameter in the Roman province of Asia (Western Turkey). Within this circle, Christ walked (Revelation 2:1).

The Church at Pergamos identifies a faithful church but one which tolerated false teachers (Revelation 2:12-17).

Pergamos Seat Of Satan

Pergamos was at the center of the province of Asia and was the place where the state religion was most thoroughly promoted, that is, the worship of emperors. Pergamos is inland and 60 miles north of Smyrna. It was the capital of Asia before this was moved to Ephesus.

Here stood a 200,000 volume library second only to that in Alexandria; and thus it is not strange that the word *parchment* is derived from the name of this city.

Here among the gods, the deity of medicine, Aesculapius, was honored *("scalpel")* . . . often with the sign of a snake. See Numbers 21:8, 9. The Caduceus, used as a symbol of the medical profession, was an outgrowth of the Tau cross. The Tau cross was inscribed on the forehead of every person admitted into the Mysteries of Mithras. From 1400 BC to 400 AD, the Persians, Romans and Greeks worshipped the god Mithras. The Romans only men were initiated into this cult. There were seven grades of initiation. These ceremonies included a baptism, the common meal (imitations of Christianity), a special handshake and being led blindfolded before the leader (later carried over by Masons).

Mithras was the god of light and truth and had his origins possibly from Plato's writings and thought. So we see that Pergamos wavered back and forth from following Christ to following Satan.

The Zeus Altar

Upon the city's acropolis stood the Temple of Athena and the great altar to Zeus, which had a base over 100 feet square. These stood 800 feet above the plains. They fittingly could be described as "Satan's Seat" (Revelation 2:13). It was here in Pergamos that three Imperial Temples were built for worshipping the Roman emperor.

Revelation 2:14 tells us more about Pergamos:

> But I have a few things against thee, because thou hast there
> them that hold the doctrine of Balaam

Babylon in all its splendor pictured at left. Today only ruins remain. Lion statue marks site of Daniel's lion's den.

The Doctrine Of Balaam

The doctrine of Balaam (Numbers, chapters 22-25) was the encouraging of Israelites to marry pagan wives. And in Pergamos, this refers to those who teach that it is permissible to mix Christianity and paganism. The Saviour comes with a sharp sword to cut these apart (Revelation 2:12). We find many church leaders today compromising the gospel by approving of marriages of believer with unbeliever. They also seek a unified church that mixes believers with modernists and cultists. This is an area today where Satan is becoming increasingly successful . . . just as he was in the days of Pergamos.

How often have you heard the cry: *"Sure, we're Christians, but everyone else does it. Do you want us to stick out like a sore thumb . . . lose our friendships?"*

Both the imperial temples devoted to the emperor and those dedicated to the gods prided themselves in holding *"secrets."* The health resorts of Pergamos also had its mysteries. How much this patterns after today's cults and secret organizations such as freemasonry!

The word *Pergamos* itself seems to be derived from: *pergos*, "tower" and *gamos*, "marriage." This makes us think of the city's tower to Athena and Zeus and to its marriage of Christianity with paganism.

Satan's Subtle Seduction

It has been said that when Satan could not drive the Church out of the world by persecution during the Smyrna period (100-313 AD), he attempted to drive the world into the Church in the Pergamos era (313-590 AD).

Satan's peril to the Church is a 3-pronged attack:

Three-Pronged Attack

1. **He is never still!**
   The Bible tells us that Satan is constantly active and warns us:

   Be sober, be vigilant;
   because your adversary the devil,
   as a roaring lion,
   walketh about,
   seeking whom he may devour.

   (1 Peter 5:8)

   If you have ever seen a roaring lion, you know he is continually pacing up and down always on the alert for his next victim!

2. **He is never full!**
   You cannot quench Satan's appetite. Again 1 Peter 5:8 reminds us that he is "seeking whom he may devour."

3. **He is cruel in his attack.**
   He is a deceiver (Revelation 12:9). He is the author of lying (John 8:44). Be sure to read Luke 8:29 and Luke 9:39.

9-Point Program

Satan has at least a 9-point program for the Church.

1. **Satan casts doubt upon the Authority of the Word of God.**
   He began his evangelistic program in the Garden of Eden when he said to Eve:

   Yea, hath God said,
   Ye shall not eat of every tree
   of the Garden?

   (Genesis 3:1)

   In the temptation of Jesus, he perverted the Scriptures by omitting a portion. Compare Matthew 4:6 with Psalm

91:11, 12. How many times, in today's world, believers when suddenly faced with a testing, seek their own solution, doubting the promises of the Word of God!

2. Satan seeks to promote false doctrine.

God warns us:

. . . in the latter times
some shall depart from the faith,
giving heed to seducing spirits,
and doctrines of devils (demons).

(1 Timothy 4:1)

These false cults will have an "anesthetized" conscience . . . put to sleep and insensitive (seared with a hot iron, 1 Timothy 4:2). They are liars, convincing ones with added secrets and new theologies that they alone are the "*last word.*"

How can we test these false cults to expose them for what they really are? God in His Word tells us exactly how!

Every spirit that confesseth not
that Jesus Christ is come in the flesh,
*   is not of God:*
and this is that spirit of antichrist,
whereof ye have heard that it should
*   come;*
and even now already is it in the
*   world.*

(1 John 4:3)

For such are false apostles,
deceitful workers,
transforming themselves
into the apostles of Christ.
And no marvel;
for Satan himself is transformed
into an angel of light.

(2 Corinthians 11:13, 14)

We, however, will have the victory if we abide in the promises of God and follow

His will because:

Greater is He that is in you,
than he (Satan) that is in the world.

(1 John 4:4)

3. **Satan seeks to capitalize on dissension in the body of Christ in the Church.**
No doubt you have been in churches and in Christian organizations where there has been highly charged disagreements and eventual splits. Many Churches exist today because they have become an offshoot of a split. One of Satan's favorite military maneuvers is to send his "*dissension angels*" into a growing, successful church and tear it apart pitting Christian against Christian.

If your Church is witnessing souls saved, a real revival of the Saints, an effective witness ... BEWARE! Be on guard. For Satan has also witnessed this. He is not satisfied with his past victories and the carnage he has brought in past battles.

If your church is on fire for God, if you are not on guard, his angels will slip in and tear your church apart ... deacon against deacon ... family against family ... congregation against pastor ... elders against people. And if he can't get victory there, he will start on the Choir!

Satan knows that just 3½ years before his imprisonment (Revelation 20:1-3) he will hear a loud voice from heaven saying:

Now is come salvation, and strength,
and the kingdom of our God,
and the power of His Christ:
for the accuser of our brethren (Satan)
is cast down,

which accused them before our God
day and night.

(Revelation 12:10)

But until that time, you can count on
him pacing back and forth in your
church as a roaring lion, seeking whom
he may devour!

4. **Satan seeks to hinder the work of
Christians.**

There are many evidences in Scripture
where Satan attempts to stop the
spreading of the Word of God. Here are a
few:

A. Gospel seed that is sown by the
wayside is snatched away by him:

*When any one heareth the Word of
the kingdom, and understandeth it
not, then cometh the wicked one
(Satan), and catcheth away that
which was sown in his heart.*

(Matthew 13:19)

B. The lost in the world are blinded by
him:

*the god of this world (Satan) hath
blinded the minds of them which
believe not, lest the light of the
glorious gospel of Christ, who is the
image of God, should shine unto
them.*

(2 Corinthians 4:4)

C. The soul winners are hindered by
him:

*Wherefore we would have come
unto you, even I Paul, once and
again; but Satan hindered us.*

(1 Thessalonians 2:18)

D. The False clergymen are active to
spread his message:

Christ reminded the crowds that evil
people will be very active in the evil

days to come. He lashed out at the Pharisees (who had a form of godliness) who claimed to be experts in religion:

Ye have taken away the key of knowledge: ye have not entered in yourselves, and them that were entering in ye hindered!

(Luke 11:52)

How active false clergymen are today! And how effective are the cults that lead innocent lambs to the slaughter! One day, they will answer for their evil deeds at the Great White Throne Judgment (Revelation 20:11, 12).

5. <u>**Satan suggests evil acts to the mind.**</u>
It was Satan who encouraged Judas to betray Jesus Christ.

And supper being ended,
the devil
having now put
into the heart of Judas Iscariot,
Simon's son to betray
Him (Christ) . . .   (John 13:2)

It was Satan that caused Ananias and his wife Sapphira to lie regarding their possessions.

But Peter said,
Ananias,
Why hath Satan filled thine heart to lie to the Holy Ghost, and to keep back part of the price of the land?

(Acts 5:3)

It was Satan that encouraged David to take a prideful census of the people of Israel!

And Satan stood up against Israel, and provoked David to number Israel.   (1 Chronicles 21:1)

6. Satan generates sexual immorality.

Not satisfied with his successes in the Garden of Eden, Satan sought to corrupt man with evil desires towards the beautiful women of that day. When the Lord saw the evil extent of human wickedness and that their hearts were filled with evil continually:

> ... the Lord was sorry that he had made man on the earth, and it grieved Him at His heart.
>
> (Genesis 6:6)

When the Pharisees (religious leaders of that day) brought to Jesus a woman caught in the act of adultery, Jesus did not condone the sin, but did forgive the sinner and told her:

> Go, and sin no more.
>
> (John 8:11)

The Pharisees, not satisfied, attempted to cast doubt that Christ was sent of God, His Father. Their hypocritical righteousness denied the Good News of salvation, and Christ, in strong language, told them (when they claimed Abraham was their father):

> Ye are of your father the devil, and the lusts of your father ye will do.
>
> (John 8:44)

7. Satan seeks to destroy marriages.

When a man and woman get married, it is a union of two people who become "one flesh" (1 Corinthians 6:16). It involves mutual obligations. A girl who marries no longer has full rights to her own life or body. In the same way, the husband no longer has full right to his own self and body, for he belongs also to his wife. See 1 Corinthians 7:4.

With this in mind, God's Word tells us:

Defraud (do not refuse) *ye not*
one the other,
except it be with consent
for a time,
that ye may give yourselves
to fasting and prayer;
and come together again
(in physical union)
that Satan tempt you not
for your incontinency
(lack of self-control).

(1 Corinthians 7:5)

Paul was aware that Satan would tempt husband and wife and cause their marriage to fall apart over some disagreements. Satan is aware that the lack of physical union among husband and wife helps to widen this split in a marriage. This is why God reminds us that when a man and woman get married, they are to become as one. To refrain from physical union (except for a time of fasting and prayer) could lead to temptations, causing one to satisfy the appetite wrongly ... and thus falling into Satan's trap!

8. Satan exploits our families and wrecks our testimonies.

Oftentimes when Satan cannot dampen the Christian testimony of the mother and father, he sows his seed of dissension among the children. And here he has most often been highly successful. How many dedicated Christian parents do you know who faithfully served God through the years now bear a burden of children who follow after Satan! These are the devil's trophies! The term "minister's children" is often a reference to irresponsible children who in no way are the pattern of their parents! Yes, Satan especially delights in attacking the children of those who are in the Lord's work full-time . . . ministers, missionaries, Christian workers! For in so doing, he hopes to undermine the work of God.

9. **Satan seeks to destroy our witness through pride.**

God's Word tells us:

Pride goeth before destruction, and an haughty spirit before a fall.

(Proverbs 16:18)

One of the sins of Sodom was her sin of pride (Ezekiel 16:49). Nebuchadnezzar's heart was lifted up and his mind was hardened in pride and because of this he lost his kingship (Daniel 5:20). Satan used the sin of pride to bring the downfall of the Philistines, Assyria and Jordan (Zechariah 9:6; 10:11; 11:3).

There are many ways Satan destroys the effectiveness of the believer by defiling him with pride. They include:

A. The pride of Prominence

How often have we seen a newborn child of God thrust suddenly into a place of popularity and prominence. A motion picture star, a football player, a famous politician . . . accepts Christ and soon finds himself in the limelight in churches, on religious television programs, in large denominational gatherings. The Bible warns us not to give responsibilities to a novice (one new in the faith)

lest he fall into reproach and the snare of the devil.

(1 Timothy 3:7)

B. The pride of Accomplishment

There is a human tendency, by our actions to say:

Look what I have accomplished. See how many souls I won to Christ! Look how large our Sunday School is! Look how successful our evangelistic campaign was! There has never been a Sunday when at least one soul did not accept Christ in our church!

These are all evidences of pride of self!

Remember this! God does not have to depend on us to make His purposes complete! We are to be grateful to Him that He allows us to be channels. Many of us allow our channels to be blocked by the boulder rocks of pride and self-praise! Too many of us strive to be the vine . . . instead of the branch. We should daily remind ourselves that without Christ . . . we can do NOTHING (John 15:5).

Three times Paul asked the Saviour to remove the thorn in the flesh. But God allowed this thorn:

. . . the messenger of Satan to buffet me, lest I should be exalted above measure.

(2 Corinthians 12:7)

Paul had no desire to encourage hero worship. The Lord allowed this divine deterrent (a thorn) in order to deflate any tendency toward exaltation in pride.

C. The pride of Separation and Exclusivism

This is perhaps the most difficult for me to write and maintain Christian grace. For more than any other weakness I have witnessed in the Christian church among believers, this weakness seems to be growing in intensity! I personally am convinced that some leaders in some groups do not know the meaning of humility nor are they familiar with the admonition:

Be kindly affectioned one to another with brotherly love; in honour preferring one another.

(Romans 12:10)

What does this mean, "... *in honour preferring one another*"? In modern English it means:

Try to outdo one another
in showing respect and honour.

Or

Take delight
in honoring each other.

All of us need improvement in this area of our Christian walk! How we need humility! If we humble ourselves, Christ will exalt us (1 Peter 5:6).

It is not a sin to be a Baptist or a Presbyterian or to be reformed! Nor is it sin to be a deacon or an elder!

But when a person dwells and dwells on his group or denomination flaunting it as his badge of "*higher holiness*," it becomes the sin of pride.

When a deacon, flushed with his sudden influential power and importance, uses his office to impose his own selfish ideas detrimental to the harmony of the church, this becomes the sin of pride.

How many times have you witnessed fractional denominationalism wreck the Christian testimony! How many times have you witnessed cliques of Christians, in their small exclusive circles, claiming that their group alone is following true Christianity! What sin of pride!

Does not Satan get us involved in devious detours to ruin our effective witness for Christ?

Victory Through God

We have covered <u>nine</u> ways Satan is trying to destroy the church. All of us should be aware of Satan's sinister plan. Victory over Satan comes when each of us follow God's directive:

> Submit yourselves therefore to God.
> Resist the devil,
> and he will flee from you.
> Draw nigh to God,
> and He will draw nigh to you.
>
> (James 4:7, 8)

That first step can start with showing brotherly love and in honor preferring one another (Romans 12:10).

30

SATAN'S FINAL DESTINY

**Satan
Is A
Defeated
Foe!**

It is with joy that I write this final chapter. For in researching the inner workings of Satan and his invisible and visible armies, it is easy for one to become discouraged over Satan's apparent victories!

But praise God . . . **Satan is a <u>defeated</u> foe!** See John 12:31. And he knows it! But before he reaches his final destiny he will attempt to create havoc throughout the world. Read your daily newspaper and you will see the footprints of Satan's army.

In Ephesian 6:12 we are warned:

> *We wrestle not against flesh and blood, but against principalities, against powers, against the rulers of the darkness of this world, against spiritual wickedness in high places.*

Satan's angels are organized into a military-like structure. Satan has a hierarchy with a group of his angels that govern, another group that is assigned specific authority and who influence leaders of human government.

Satan Influences World Events

Satan can and does influence world events. Daniel had prayed for three weeks seeking God's favor upon the Jewish people in rebuilding the Temple. The angel had left Heaven immediately after Daniel's first prayer but on his way to earth he had encountered opposition from *"the prince of the kingdom of Persia"* (Daniel 10:12, 13). God sent Michael, the archangel, to pave the way for God's answer to Daniel's prayer.

The rulers of Persia (now Iran) were hindering the Jews from rebuilding the Temple. All the people of Jerusalem could see was the evident treachery of their human enemies. But they did not realize they were also fighting an invisible army . . . directed by Satan. It took 3 weeks for Daniel's prayer to be answered because of the war in the heavens! See Revelation 12:7 and Daniel 12:1.

Even today, we see evidence that men who hold high political office may be the unwitting tools of Satan's invisible army of angels! We see Satan's victories when men in power tell lies, when they oppress others, when they commit mass murders via war or economic starvation. Oddly enough, in this refined, sophisticated, modernized, affluent society . . . we are witnessing more inhumanity of man upon man than in ancient barbaric times.

Satan's Power Is Limited

As powerful as Satan is, there are limitations to his power.

1. **Satan is limited by God's omnipotence.**
   Our Lord and Saviour is in ultimate control of this world. In the book of Job we are reminded that Satan could do only what God allowed (Job 1:12; 2:6). Paul reminds us that earthly rulers only have authority because of God's permissive decree.

   Let every soul be subject unto the higher powers. For there is no power but of God; the powers that be are ordained of God.

   (Romans 13:1)

2. **Satan is restricted by the presence of Christians.**
   Believers exercise a purifying effect upon the world and exert a strong influence in world action. The advent of Christian television programming and a large Christian majority particularly in the United States, has had a stablizing effect. This has limited Satan's victories. Jesus reminds us:

   Ye are the salt of the earth.

   (Matthew 5:13)

   Salt does have a purifying and cleansing effect. Because Christians are indwelt with the Holy Spirit, the full venting of Satan's fury is hindered (2 Thessalonians 2:6, 7).

3. **Satan is limited by his ultimate destiny.**
   Satan is working under a severe handicap. He knows that his ultimate destiny is defeat. He knows his doom is sure, and that he is definitely limited (Revelation 12:12).

Satan's Control

Don't be lulled into a self-complacency, however. **Satan still has power over the wicked on this earth.**

1. They are his children.
(Acts 13:10, 1 John 3:10)
2. They do his will.
(John 8:44)
3. Satan possesses them.
(Luke 22:3)
4. Satan blinds them!
(2 Corinthians 4:4)
5. Satan blinds them.
(Revelation 20:7, 8)
6. He traps them.
(1 Timothy 3:7)
7. Satan deceives them.
(1 Samuel 16:14)

Then too, of course, the wicked are punished along with Satan (Matthew 25:41).

Satan has power to affect God's people.

1. Satan tempts them.
(1 Chronicles 21:1)
2. Satan afflicts them.
(Job 1:12)
3. Satan opposes them.
(Zechariah 3:1)
4. Satan sifts them.
(Luke 22:31)
5. Satan fools them.
(2 Corinthians 11:3)

Christ's triumph over Satan is:

1. Predicted (Genesis 3:15)
2. Portrayed (Matthew 4:4-11)
3. Proclaimed (Luke 10:18)
4. Perfected (Mark 3:27)

Satan's greatest triumph over Christians is to divert the worship that belongs to God on to himself!

Works Of Satan

And he accomplishes this through subtle means that appear within the realm of the *"acceptable"* among Christians. Here are a few examples you may not have realized are the works of Satan.

1. **Materialism above missions.**

   In most areas of the world, a majority of Christians are blessed materially. In the United States most people have television sets, automobiles, telephones and eat 3 meals a day. The government assures us all types of security from social security to medicare and medicaid. There is a dangerous tendency among Christians to proportionately spend more on themselves *"to maintain their station in life"* and to *"retain the conveniences to which we are accustomed."* This is done at the expense of giving sacrificially to worthy missionary organizations. The highest percentage of giving, in fact, goes to large popularized ministries whose basic ministry is overstuffing, overstuffed Christians.

2. **Pleasure over prayer.**

   Prayer meetings in churches in America are, for the most part, a relic of the past. A church may get 800 to its Sunday morning service but only 30 out to prayer meeting. Many, many fundamental churches have abandoned prayer meeting. The history of the church's progress is the history of prayer. John R. Rice wisely reminds us: *"The Bible doesn't say we should preach all the time, but it does say we should pray all the time."* Satan has used the lusts of pleasure to seduce us away from the power of prayer! This certainly is a mark of the end of this age!

From their programming, it is evident that many churches are more interested in entertaining Christians and playing war games. What they fail to realize is that we are at WAR . . . and the time for war games has long since passed!

3. Division over Dedication.

Perhaps one of Satan's greatest delights is in causing divisions within the church. How often Christian leaders, who have their own hobby horses, push their beliefs and convictions to the point where they cause divisions. One can disagree without being disagreeable. There are times we become so denominationally oriented that many wonder whether one is more interested in a partisan cause rather than Christ. Sometimes we become guilty of creating an *"exclusivism"* within our own little circle. Let us, including myself, determine to dedicate our life to Christ and not fall prey to Satan's power play of division!

The False Trinity

There are three major leaders during the Tribulation Period of 7 years: **Antichrist** (the world leader), the **False Prophet** (the world religious leader) and their director, **Satan.** This is the False Trinity which attempts to imitate the work of God the Fa-

ther, Christ the Son, and the Holy Spirit (Revelation 15:13).

The final end for Antichrist and the False Prophet comes at the end of the 7-year Tribulation Period after the Battle of Armageddon. Antichrist, whose 42 months of world power began when he desecrated the Temple in Jerusalem in the middle of the 7-year Tribulation Period, now must face the consequences of his sins. He is cast into the Lake of Fire (Revelation 19:20).

The False Prophet, the religious leader who directed allegiance to Antichrist, is also cast into the Lake of Fire (Revelation 19:20).

They are not merely slain . . . as the multitudes are who took part in the Battle of Armageddon. Both of these masterminds of iniquity are actually cast **alive** into the Lake of Fire without waiting for any final judgment. The Lake of Fire is the place of eternal suffering burning with brimstone, a place of perpetual darkness with no hope of deliverance.

Satan, at this period of time, is bound in the bottomless pit for 1000 years. He does not reappear until the end of the 1000 year Millennium. The bottomless pit is not necessarily Hades or Hell but a holding place where Satan is bound in some type of spirit-world chains (see Revelation 20:1-3).

At the end of the 1000 year Millennium Satan is given one final brief opportunity to call upon people to follow him.

Millennium Believers

There are **two** types of Believers living in the Millennium period:

1. **Resurrected Believers**
   Those previously resurrected at the Rapture and those saints who died in the Tribulation and were resurrected along with Old Testament saints. They will be given positions of responsibility (Matthew 19:28; Luke 19:12-27).

2. **Living Believers**
   Gentiles and Jews alike who are still living at the close of the Battle of Armageddon, and who are permitted to enter the Millennial Kingdom. They were not raptured, nor did they die in the Tribulation Period. They are still in their human, unresurrected bodies.

During the Millennium, these **Living Believers** will still be fully normal people who are able to reproduce children. These children will still be born with a sin nature. For them, as for all humans born at any time, salvation is still required. They must individually make a decision whether to accept Jesus Christ as Saviour and Lord . . . or to deny Him.

Satan Released

At the end of the 1000 year Millennium Satan is released to gather the unbelievers to battle against the Lord and the believers. (Remember, these unbelievers are those born during the Millennium who decide not to accept Christ as Saviour and Lord even though they have lived a life of 1000 years of peace and prosperity!)

How many decide to follow Satan? As many as ". . . *the sand of the sea*" (Revelation 20:8). This could involve several millions of people, even though this might be only a tiny minority in the Millennial world. This vast number of people will completely encircle the Living Believers within the capital city of Jerusalem in a state of siege.

This becomes a battle where God destroys the wicked supernaturally . . . it is another Battle of Gog and Magog (Revelation 20:7-10). This is an *anti-Christ* onslaught by people gathered from *all over the earth.* (Do not confuse this with the original Battle of Gog and Magog of Ezekiel 38:1-39:16. This is an *anti-Israel* invasion from the *north* directed by Russia).

In Genesis 3, Satan deceived our first parents, Adam and Eve, into believing that they could rebel against God, and by so doing, improve their lot. He also scoffed at their incurring the awful promised penalty of death for their sin.

The Final Rebellion

So, too, at the end of the 1000 year Millennium, Satan will somehow, by some means, lure some thousands or millions into rebellion against Christ. When this occurs, God brings fire down from Heaven killing Satan's entire army (Revelation 20:9). Satan is then cast into the Lake of Fire where Antichrist and the False Prophet already are (Revelation 20:10).

After this occurs the **Great White Throne Judgment.** This is the final judgment of the unsaved, non-believers, of **all** of the ages. These are resurrected for this event and they are judged before God (Revelation 20:11-15).

While they followed Satan they anticipated a sweet victory. They looked forward to the ultimate in the fruits of the flesh. Now, finally, they will discover that Satan is defeated and their anticipated fruits have soured into bitter judgment.

The dictators, the kings, the presidents who oppressed their people, who killed and lusted for power . . . the millions of people who followed Satan and denied Christ . . . the religious leaders who had a form of godliness but denied its power . . . now reach the end of the road!

Saddest Roll Call In History!

Here is the saddest roll call in history! No matter how wealthy or powerful you are in today's world . . . you will not be able to buy or influence your way into Heaven. No matter how many good works you did on earth . . . to God they are as *"filthy rags"* (Isaiah 64:6).

All unbelievers are cast into the Lake of Fire (Revelation 20:15). Thus ends . . . and begins . . . the most tragic moment in history! Here begins that moment for the unbeliever which starts an eternity in constant torment and eternal separation from God, called by the Bible, *"the Second Death"* (Revelation 20:14).

Perhaps, as you read this, you don't believe it. But think about this for a moment. Satan and his angels believe it! Turn to James 2:19 in the New Testament:

. . . *the devils also believe and* <u>*tremble*</u>.

If Satan and his angels believe . . . and in believing . . . tremble . . . should you any less believe that when God says something . . . He means it!

Right now, Satan and his host of angels (demons) are fighting a losing war. They know the outcome. As that outcome comes closer they will become more vicious in their determination to win as many converts as possible.

One of the names of Satan is Apollyon (or Abaddon—Revelation 9:11). This means: *one who exterminates!* Under Satan's leadership his demon angels are very active seeking to wipe out the purposes of God. How many demon angels are there? We do not know. They may equal or exceed in number the number of the total population of the earth at any given time. The demons not only work in the ordinary realms but are especially active in the political and religious realms. The recent growth of many cults as well as world atheistic communism is evidence of this.

In Ephesians 2:2, God's Word tells us that Satan is:

the prince of the power of the air . . .

What a joy for believers to realize that at the Rapture Jesus Christ will pierce Satan's domain and:

we . . . shall be caught up . . . in the clouds to meet the Lord in the air; and so shall we ever be with the Lord.

(1 Thessalonians 4:16, 17)

And death and hell were cast into the lake of fire. This is the second death. And whosoever was not found written in the book of life was cast into the lake of fire.

(Revelation 20:14,15)

Satan cannot have ultimate power over the believer! Praise God! We will break through his domain to be ever with the Lord!

The Lake of Fire need not be your destiny. Jesus Christ offered Himself as a sacrifice for sin to bring you to God.

Tragic Destiny

Satan's angels do not have this opportunity. They are destined for the Lake of Fire! They have no hope, no promise of salvation.

But God, in grace *(unmerited favor)* has offered salvation to you. However, the decision is yours. Will you choose Heaven or the Lake of Fire? Will you choose Jesus Christ or Satan?

You have read of Satan's plan and Satan's program. You now know Satan's final position . . . an eternity in the Lake of Fire.

You are now aware that Satan has a visible army and countless invisible angels (demons) who carry out his purposes. It is my prayer that this book will assist in turning you from sin to salvation, from following Satan to following the Saviour . . . now that you have seen Satan's angels EXPOSED!

The Characteristics of Hell
THE FIRE THAT NEVER SHALL BE QUENCHED

Many people jokingly refer to Hell as a place where they will be busy greeting all their friends. Unfortunately, this if far from the Scriptural picture, in the sense that they will not be greeting their friends but rather, they will be in eternal torment.

All the non-believers, with Satan, with Antichrist and with the False Prophet and Satan's angels will be together in the final Lake of Fire.

Hell will be:

1. A PLACE OF CONSCIOUSNESS

You will recall in Scriptures a message concerning a certain rich man and Lazarus, a beggar. The rich man was conscious in Hell and he was in torment:

> *And in Hades* (the realm of the dead, Hell), *being in torment, he lifted up his eyes ... and cried out ...*
>
> *(Luke 16:23,24)*

This Scripture indicates that the unsaved dead are CONSCIOUS.

2. A PLACE OF TORMENT

Both in the above verse just quoted and in verse 28 of Luke 16:

> *... warn them* (the rich man's 5 brothers) *... lest they too come into this place of torment.*

we have an indication from God that Hell is a real place of torment. Also Hell, from these Scriptures, is shown as a hot place for the rich man asks that Lazarus (the beggar who went to Heaven) *"dip the tip of his finger in water and cool my tongue; for I am in anguish in this flame"* (Luke 16:24).

Can you imagine the intense suffering from an unbearable heat? Anyone who has been to Vietnam or other hot climates, where the suffocating humidity envelops you along with the intense heat, can visualize this scene.

Also picture the desperateness of the occasion when the rich man would welcome the beggar Lazarus to get water on his finger to alleviate the suffering!

Hell is truly a place of real torment!

3. A PLACE OF DARKNESS

We are told in Matthew that the unsaved

> *... will be driven out into the darkness outside, where there will be weeping and grinding of teeth.*
>
> *(Matthew 8:12)*

Also

> *... throw him* (the unsaved) *into the darkness outside* (of Heaven); *there will be weeping and grinding of teeth.*
>
> *(Matthew 22:13)*

And in Jude 13 we are told that the *"gloom of darkness"* has been *"reserved forever"* for those outside of Christ. What a picture of hopelessness!

4. ETERNAL SEPARATION FROM LOVED ONES

Think about this for a moment. If you are an unbeliever and some of your best friends and loved relatives (perhaps even a husband or wife) are BELIEVERS ... they will go to Heaven ... and you will be eternally separated from them!

> There shall be weeping and gnashing of teeth, when ye shall see Abraham, and Isaac, and Jacob, and all the prophets, in the kingdom of God, and you yourselves thrust out.
>
> (Luke 13:28)

What a tragedy to enter Hell and then to realize that you are now eternally separated from those whom you loved so much on this earth!

5. NOT THE SLIGHTEST HOPE OF RELEASE

Many places in Scripture tell of Hell being a place of eternal judgment from which there is no turning back. In Hebrews 6:2 we learn that Hell is a place of "eternal judgment." In Matthew 25:46 it is revealed that the unbeliever will "go away into everlasting punishment...."

6. THE TORMENT OF MEMORY IN HELL

This, perhaps could be the most agonizing aspect of those in Hell ... the torment of a memory ... a memory that will evoke continual anguish. This is brought out so clearly in Luke 16:27,28 where the rich man implores Abraham to:

> ... send him (Lazarus, who is in Heaven) to my father's house: For I have five brethren; that he may testify unto them, lest they also come into this place of torment.
>
> (Luke 16:27,28)

What an insight into Hell! Imagine if those unsaved dead right now could speak to us for just a moment ... what a warning they would give ... and yet, sad to say, would anyone pay attention?

How pointedly Abraham replied ... and how prophetically when he said,

> ... If they hear not Moses and the prophets, neither will they be persuaded, **though one rose from the dead.**
>
> (Luke 16:31)

Thus, the unbeliever in Hell must go through an eternity in torment with a searing, ever-present memory!

7. THE TORMENT OF UNSATISFIED LUSTFUL CRAVINGS

In Hell the unbeliever will **never gain satisfaction.** Sin will continue in Hell but it will be a constant craving ... without fulfilling. Thus we read,

> He who is unrighteous (unjust, wicked) let him be unrighteous still, and he that is filthy (vile, impure) let him be filthy still....
>
> (Revelation 22:11)

These words here are referring to the activity in Hell. Can you imagine the surprise that awaits the filth peddlers who on this earth are having a heyday distributing pornographic films and literature?

At least, here on earth this activity brings them barrels of cash while they influence negatively the lives of others.

But in Hell, these filth peddlers will have their cravings and lusts ... but these will be unfulfilled cravings. Can you imagine the intensity of suffering this will cause!

WHAT WILL YOU DO WITH JESUS?

After reading SATAN'S ANGELS EXPOSED it should become evident to you that Satan has a deceptive plan to capture your soul! You cannot simply ignore him. You must make a decision. What happens when it comes time for you to depart from this earth?

Then WHAT WILL YOU DO WITH JESUS?

Here are five basic observations in the Bible of which you should be aware:

1. *ALL SIN — For all have sinned, and come short of the glory of God.* (Romans 3:23)

2. *ALL LOVED — For God so loved the world, that He gave His only begotten Son, that whosoever believeth in Him should not perish, but have everlasting life.* (John 3:16)

3. *ALL RAISED — Marvel not at this: for the hour is coming, in which all that are in the graves shall hear his voice. And shall come forth; they that have done good, unto the resurrection of life; and they that have done evil, unto the resurrection of damnation.* (John 5:28,29)

4. *ALL JUDGED — . . . we shall all stand before the judgment seat of Christ.* (Romans 14:10)
   And I saw the dead, small and great, stand before God; and the books were opened. . . (Revelation 20:12)

5. *ALL BOW — . . . at the name of Jesus every knee should bow. . .*
   (Philippians 2:10)

Right now, in simple faith, you can have the wonderful assurance of eternal life.

Ask yourself, honestly, the question. . . . WHAT WILL I DO WITH JESUS?

God tells us the following:

". . .him that cometh to me I will in no wise cast out. (37) *Verily, verily (truly) I say unto you, He that believeth on me (Christ) hath everlasting life"* (47)—(John 6:37, 47).

He also is a righteous God and a God of indignation to those who reject Him. . . .

". . .he that believeth not is condemned already, because he hath not believed in the name of the only begotten Son of God."
(John 3:18)

"And whosoever was not found written in the book of life was cast into the lake of fire"—(Revelation 20:15).

YOUR MOST IMPORTANT DECISION IN LIFE

All of your riches here on earth—all of your financial security—all of your material wealth, your houses, your land will crumble into nothingness in a few years.

No matter how great your works—no matter how kind you are—no matter how philanthropic you are—it means nothing in the sight of God, because in the sight of God, your riches are as filthy rags.

"...all our righteousness are as filthy rags..."

(Isaiah 64:6)

Christ expects you to come as your are, a sinner, recognizing your need of a Saviour, the Lord Jesus Christ.

Understanding this, why not bow your head right now and give this simple prayer of faith to the Lord.

My Personal Decision for CHRIST

"Lord Jesus, I know that I'm a sinner and that I cannot save myself by good works. I believe that you died for me and that you shed your blood for my sins. I believe that you rose again from the dead. And now I am receiving you as my personal Saviour, my Lord, my only hope of salvation. I know that I cannot save myself, Lord, be merciful to me, a sinner, and save me according to the promise of Your Word. I want Christ to come into my heart now to be my Saviour, Lord and Master."

Signed ....

Date ....

If you have signed the above, having just taken Christ as your personal Saviour and Lord...I would like to rejoice with you in your new found faith.

Write to me...Salem Kirban, 604 Mason's Mill Road, Huntingdon Valley, Penna. 19006...and I'll send you a little booklet to help you start living your new life in Christ.

EDGAR CAYCE and ASSOCIATION for RESEARCH and ENLIGHTENMENT, INC. (A.R.E.)

Background

Edgar Cayce (pronounced Casey) was born near Hopkinsville, Kentucky in 1877. It was reported that his grandfather had psychic power because he could **"make a broom dance"** and was able to locate underground water sources by dowsing.

Edgar was an avid Bible reader and Sunday School teacher. His son, Hugh, claims that his father was able to sleep with his head on his schoolbooks and absorb the information via a photographic memory. He was able to advance rapidly through school. (*Author's* note: I would not suggest today's student try this. The only thing he will get is a stiff neck.)

Cayce quit school early to work and eventually became a salesman for a wholesale stationery company. It was at this time that he developed a paralysis of his throat muscles. Doctors were unable to help him. Finally his friend, Al Layne, helped Cayce to go into a trance (as he had done in childhood days). In this unconscious state Cayce gave his first **"reading"** in which he recommended medication and manipulative therapy. His voice was successfully restored.

Cayce entered his sleep-like state at least 16,000 times during his lifetime . . . recommended physical cures through his trance **"readings."** Many followed his trance information claiming healing. Newspapers reported of his successes. This caught the eye of Arthur Lammers who was a wealthy printer from Dayton, Ohio.

Lammers had interests differing from Cayce. Lammers was into metaphysics, astrology, psychic phenomena, the cabala, yoga, theosophy and the Great White Brotherhood. Lammers also believed in reincarnation. He was able to convince Cayce to give him some **"readings"** on these sub-jects to gain support for them. Cayce was amazed when his **"readings"** agreed with these non-Biblical doctrines. When he was told what he said while in a trance concerning rein-carnation and astrology, he remarked to Lammers:

> *What you have been telling me today, and*
> *what the readings have been saying,*
> *is foreign to all I've believed and been taught,*
> *and all I've taught to others, all my life.*
> *If ever the Devil was going to play a trick on me,*
> *this would be it.*

(<u>There is a River</u>, p. 210)

It was at this point Cayce was swayed by Lammers and he turned away from the literal interpretation of the Bible. He placed more faith in his "readings" than in the Word of God. He firmly believed that the "readings" did not lie.

In 1925 Cayce moved to Virginia Beach, Virginia. In 1928 he founded the Cayce Hospital for Research and Enlighten-ment. This hospital was lost during the depression of the

Some of the many books on Edgar Cayce, former Sunday School teacher who created his own occult philosophy.

1930's and repurchased in 1956. It is now the headquarters of Cayce's **A.R.E.** (Association for Research and Enlightenment). Cayce died in 1945 and his son, Hugh Lynn, took the reins of the A.R.E. At that time there were only about 700 members.

Beliefs

In his book, _Cults and the Occult in the Age of Aquarius_, Edmond C. Gruss writes:

> Those who write about Edgar Cayce do not question his honesty, sincerity, motives or humanitarian goals, but Bible-believing Christians reject his psychic readings because they are often diametrically opposed to orthodox Christianity. Acceptance of Cayce's psychic "enlightenment" requires a denial of the Person and Work of Jesus Christ as well as other Christian teachings . . . [1]

Edgar Cayce's approximately 16,000 "readings" comprise about 49,000 pages of material. These "readings" were made while under a self-induced hypnotic sleep-state. About 9000 readings dealt with physical problems. The balance covered problems of life and dream interpretations. The 2500 "life readings" were given for some 1600 people and many contained references to the legendary Atlantis.

Among Cayce's readings comes forth this strange theology:

> Jesus was Adam and he learned he would be the Saviour when he fell in the Garden of Eden.

> Jesus possibly had some 30 incarnations during His development in becoming the Christ.

> Luke was written by Lucius, not Luke.

> (Lucius was Edgar Cayce in a previous incarnation, according to a Cayce "reading" and he was a companion of Christ.)

---

[1] Edmond C. Gruss, _Cults and the Occult in the Age of Aquarius_ (Grand Rapids, Michigan: Baker Book House, 1974), p. 113.

Cayce theology denies the deity of Christ and His vicarious atonement for salvation. Cayce and A.R.E. are firm believers in reincarnation.

Cayce's theology is a strange mixture of Eastern religions, of spiritualism, the mystery religions of Egypt and Persia and psychic healers.

Method of Operation

A.R.E. headquarters in Virginia Beach, Virginia draws thousands to its doors annually. Paid membership is estimated at over 50,000 with book sales averaging almost one-quarter million each year. There are approximately 2000 "Search for God" groups who meet in the U.S. and in other countries. A.R.E. Press publishes _A.R.E. Journal_ and a children's magazine called _Treasure Trove_. A.R.E. holds conferences and workshops. They run summer youth camps. They offer courses through their Atlantic University. They also maintain a medical division in Phoenix, Arizona.

THE CHILDREN OF GOD

Background

The year was 1968. Americans were engaged in the Vietnam War. Many young people were disillusioned with the war. In Huntington Beach, California, a Teen Challenge coffee house changed hands. David Berg, a former Christian and Missionary Alliance minister, took over the coffee house along with his family. Berg condemned churches as a "System" and advocated communal living. Within a short time he had 50 devoted disciples. He called his group "Teens for Christ."

Children of God demonstrate near the United Nations building in New York carrying placards warning of the impending judgment of God.

Berg claimed to be *"God's prophet for these last days."* Twice he predicted California would drop into the Pacific Ocean. He was wrong both times. He urged his followers to leave California and to make new converts around the nation. In early 1969 his followers reunited at a meeting in Texas. Berg convinced them they were like the people of Israel who wandered in the wilderness. David Berg then changed his name to Moses David and the communes were given Biblical names.

Berg then changed the name of his group to *"Children of God"* (COG). By 1975 Children of God had spread to most countries in Europe, and has since spread to about 70 countries. Most followers, however, are Americans. Estimates of the faithful number between 3000 to 5000 in about 300 small communes.

Beliefs

Berg's basic theology is that *"the end justifies the means."* Immorality—judged by traditional Christian standards—is an important part of the Children of God program. Berg (alias Moses David) states:

> We have a sexy God, and a sexy religion, and a very sexy leader with an extremely sexy young following. So, if you don't like sex, you'd better get out while you can.

Berg's theology includes forsaking all and turning it over to the Children of God! Then, as a Children of God member, you become one of the 144,000 faithful who survive the Tribulation Period. All of COG theology is centered on the End Times which he claims will end in 1993. This time-table is outlined in Berg's communication he calls his **"Mo"** Letter, No. 156, titled: *"The 70-Years Prophecy of the End."*

Children of God have no standard form of worship. They are anti-establishment Churches. Their worship consists mainly of singing, dancing, handclapping and a liturgy.

Berg is very much anti-parents! He blasts away at parents stating that one's natural family is evil and wicked:

You parents are the most God defying,
commandment breaking,
insanely rebellious rebels of all time
who are on the brink of
destroying and polluting all of us . . .
To Hell with your devilish system.
May God damn
your unbelieving hearts.

(From an early *"Mo"* letter)

Berg teaches his followers that all will be saved, including Satan himself.

Method of Operation

Children of God emphasize literature distribution. In 1970, David Berg began his bi-weekly letters to his followers. They became known as the *"Mo"* letters (short for Moses David, his new name). They are crudely written, pornographic and radical.

Children of God devotees spend 3-6 hours a day "litnessing." "Litnessing" is the term for COG witness with literature. Those who excel in *"litnessing"* are called *"shiners."* Those who fail to measure up to expectations are called *"shamers."*

Bible study is conducted in the morning and distributing literature is reserved for the afternoon.

Recruiting new members is directed towards young people, particularly on college campuses. They are invited to dinner, shown warmth and love with plenty of Scripture being quoted . . . singing, dancing, handclapping.

When an individual joins Children of God, he signs an agreement giving all his possessions and income (past, present and future) to the cult. Followers are schooled on how to write home to their parents for more money, cameras,

Two of the booklets published by Moses David's Children of God. In the booklet, "The Comet Comes," Moses David claims the Comet Kohoutek will bring impending doom and the Second Coming of Christ.

Children of God parade through Paris street near Notre Dame.

tape recorders, anything of value. Many parents falsely believe they are contributing to a Christian cause. Largest
portion of income comes from *"litnessing."* A COG member
averages $40 a day in literature sales. In one year over $5
million was raised this way.

When one first enters the *"family"* he is called a *"babe."*
After 3 months you enter Leadership Training (LT). Further
promotions include: Leader, Shepherd, Colony Shepherd
and District Shepherd.

Guru Maharaj Ji of Divine Light Mission.

DIVINE LIGHT MISSION

Background

Divine Light Mission was founded by Paran Sant Sat-gurudev Shri Hans Ji Maharaj in India. He ran a school of yoga called Siddha Yoga. He died in 1965 and his eight year old son, Maharaj Ji, became leader. This boy leader attracted world attention when he claimed he was going to establish peace in the world.

He brought his religion to the United States in July, 1971. Divine Light headquarters are in Denver, Colorado. In May, 1974, at 17, he married a follower. His life-style of expensive cars, dancing, drinking and eating meat caused a split with his family back in India. Active U.S. membership is estimated at below 10,000.

Beliefs

God has appeared through history in many incarnations. Sometimes he is personal; sometimes, impersonal.

Maharaj Ji has replaced Jesus Christ as *"the Word made flesh"* in John 1. Ji is the fullness of divine love. Unity in human life is attained by the help of Ji and the Divine Light Mission system of meditation.

Method of Operation

His followers are called *"premies."* They recruit their friends to hear satsangs (holy discourses).

The cult is spread through personal contact, through their newspaper and magazine and through films. New converts are brainwashed with intense indoctrination.

The devotees live together communally and are expected to give unquestioned devotion to Maharaj Ji.

Hare Krishna mural on stages of man seeks to emphasize reincarnation. Hare Krishna is anti-family.

Hare Krishna followers dance in Minneapolis street.

HARE KRISHNA

Background

Hare Krishna originated in India with a Hindu sect led by Lord Chaitanya. Krishna is one of the many gods in Hindu myths. Thousands of Indians believe that a Hindu born in 1865 was the promised reincarnation of a saint, and the embodiment of the god Krishna. His name: Sri Haranath, he died May, 1927.

Abhay Charan De Bhaktivedanta Swami Prabhupada, a businessman for 30 years in India, believed he was chosen to preach the Krishna message in English. He arrived in New York in 1965 and began his work in Greenwich Village by public chantings.

He published a magazine, Back To Godhead, and his influence spread to San Francisco. Krishna centers have now spread throughout the world.

Beliefs

Krishna regulations include such items as: no gambling; no sports; no conversations not associated with Krishna; no alcohol; no drugs; no tobacco; no tea; no coffee; no meat; no fish; and no eggs. For married devotees, sex only at time of full moon by permission of *"spiritual master,"* and that for having a child only.

The main purpose of life is Krishna consciousness. To attain this, chanting the Hare Krishna mantra (repetitive phrase) is demanded. Hare Krishna is anti-family. Prabhupada himself renounced and left his wife and five children to bring the movement to America.

Hare Krishna is intolerant of other faiths and demands:

> Abandon all varieties of religions
> and just surrender unto me.
>
> (Krishna quoted in the Bhagavad-Gita As It Is,
> Chapter 18, Text 66, p. 835.)

Method of Operation

Officially they are known as the International Society for Krishna Consciousness (ISKCON).

Followers live in temples under a strict Hindu cultural code. There are about 30 temples in the United States and about 40 in the rest of the world.

Money is raised through selling Back To Godhead magazine and solicitation in public places such as airports.

Devotees have an obsession with cleanliness often taking several showers a day. The primary daily activity is chanting and singing on the sidewalks (sankirtana) or selling the Krishna magazine. Each solicitor has to make a daily report of sales. They average $60 to $100 a day.

Full membership in the cult is attained in four distinct stages: (1) Temple service for about 6 months, (2) Harernama or holy name initiation rites, (3) After an additional 6 months, the brahminical initiation where a secret mantra is given you, and (4) A renunciation stage especially reserved for devoted men. It entails a life-long vow of poverty and celibacy.

THE LOCAL CHURCH

Background

This movement had its beginning in the 1940's in China. It was called the Little Flock movement but eventually became known as *"The Local Church."*

The late outstanding Christian, Watchman Nee, could be considered the originator of this group **prior** to its being highly organized and diverted in its theology. Chinese Christians, after World War 2, were looking for a *"home grown"* church. Some had become disenchanted with Western missionaries.

Watchman Nee's ministry filled this void, but Nee was not *"an organizer."* In the late 1940's Witness Lee took over as an efficient organizer. With the Communists swiftly taking over China, Watchman Nee sent Witness Lee to Formosa in 1948. The Little Flock grew to about 23,000 followers by 1955.

In 1958 Witness Lee came to the United States. Here he contacted the Chinese-speaking Local Church in San Francisco. He also met with a Los Angeles group called Westmorland Chapel.

Lee returned to the United States in 1960 on another evangelistic tour. At this point few people really knew what Lee's theological position was. Even the Navigators had him at their headquarters, because of his past association with Watchman Nee.

In 1962 the Westmorland Chapel split and Witness Lee took charge of the dissident group. Growth was slow but steady and Lee was able to indoctrinate Christians from existing fundamental churches into his cult. Its annual conference grew from 70 attendees in 1962 to 1300 in 1970.

At present it is estimated there are about 5000 members in the United States, and about 35,000 worldwide.

Beliefs

As with many successful cults, they hover back and forth from truth to error to truth thus deceiving many, Jack Sparks states:

> . . . *Local Church doctrine*
> *has an unusually great number*
> *of contradictions*
> *and inconsistencies.*
> *It wiggles all over the place . . .*
> *Local Church theology starts out*
> *innocently enough,*
> *but gets quickly off the track.*[1]

The Local Church considers established Christianity as Babylon. It, the established church, offers nothing but death. It is the great whore of the Book of Revelation, chapter 17. Thus, according to The Local Church, Christians must get out and join their movement. You cannot be a member of a local church. Their theology stresses that there is only ONE Local Church in a community that is true. Its name is THE Local Church!

Like other cults, it tries to control the mind of the individual through subtle brainwashing.

Like the Hare Krishna cult, they recite a mantra, a sort of magical chant. They would not call their phraseology a mantra . . . yet, in effect, it is. Witness Lee has this to say

---

[1] Jack Sparks, The Mind Benders (Nashville: Thomas Nelson, Inc., 1977), p. 223.

about The Local Church chant:

> *We have seen*
> *that to reach the unbelievers,*
> *no preaching is necessary.*
>
> *If we help them to say*
> *O Lord*
> *three times,*
> *they will be saved.*
>
> *All they have to do*
> *is to open their mouths*
> *and say*
> *O Lord, O Lord.*
> *Even if they have no intention*
> *of believing,*
> *still they will be caught!*[1]

Witness Lee encourages his followers to *"breathe in God and exhale the four syllables 'O Lord Jesus.' "* This becomes a powerful chant when 100 or 1000 of his followers chant this over and over again. Lee says this is *"calling upon the Lord,"* but in effect it becomes simply a repetitious chant. In support of his theology, Witness Lee has said:

> *. . . whenever we say*
> *Lord Jesus*
> *in a real way,*
> *it means that you are*
> *in the Spirit . . .*
>
> *We all have to learn to say*
> *Lord Jesus*
> *in the meeting*
> *in our home,*
> *and a thousand times a day . . .*
>
> *I tell you,*
> *you can become holy,*
> *just by saying*
> *Lord Jesus.*
> *Whenever you say*
> *Lord Jesus,*
> *you are in the Holy Spirit.* [2]

---

[1] The Stream, Vol. 8, No. 1, February 1, 1970, p. 6.

[2] Witness Lee, How To Meet (Los Angeles: Stream Publisher, 1969), p. 84.

This repetitive, mind-saturation chant also extends to what Witness Lee calls "*pray-reading.*" Lee introduced this in Taiwan in the late 1950's and it is now practiced by his followers worldwide.

In "*pray-reading*" you are not to think what you are reading. You are simply to keep your mouth going, saying whatever comes to your mind as you pore over Scriptures. By doing this, Lee says, you partake of God's very nature because "*All Scripture is God-breathed . . .*" (2 Timothy 3:16).

Here is a simulated sample of what "*pray-reading*" patterns follow. Let's assume that the Witness Lee follower is "pray-reading" John 3:16.

> *For God so loved the world,*
> > *Praise God for loving the world!*
> > *Thank you Jesus for loving me!*
> > *Amen, Lord Jesus!*
> *That He gave His only begotten Son,*
> > *Praise you Lord for your Gift!*
> > *Hallelujah Lord Jesus!*
> *That whosoever believeth in Him*
> > *Yes, Lord Jesus, I believe!*
> > *Whosoever . . . Hallelujah!*
> > *Amen! That's me! Hallelujah!*
> *Should not perish,*
> > *Thank you Lord Jesus!*
> > *Crucified with Christ and Risen!*
> > *Hallelujah, praise His name!*
> > *Amen, Lord Jesus!*
> *But have everlasting life.*
> > *Everlasting and everlasting!*
> > *I come, Lord Jesus, I come!*
> > *Hallelujah! Everlasting!*
> > *Praise You Jesus! Amen!*

While the above in itself seems fine, in this constant "*O Lord Jesus*" chant and the daily "*pray-reading*" Lee's followers get no true spiritual depth but, in effect, become automated and saturated robots following their leader. Lee's theology becomes their theology. Lee's interpretations are correct. All others are false. The Local Church becomes the supreme church.

Witness Lee encourages conformity. The individual personality must be submerged and blended into the corporate whole. Individuals strive for group recognition and acceptance.

According to Witness Lee when man fell in the Garden of Eden, he was not simply tempted and influenced by Satan from then on . . . but an actual union with Satan took place. Lee calls this "mingling." His definition of "mingling" is that:

> Mingling
> is much more
>   than mixing together;
> it is an
> intrinsic union.[1]

Thus, in Lee's theology, man and Satan became as one. Man is Satan! Lee believes that only the body and soul became united with Satan at the Fall, but the human spirit died or ceased to function.

Thus Satan dwells in the body.

The intrinsic union makes the soul into Satan.

The spirit is dead!

Lee then says:

> Regeneration
>   is the mingling of God, Himself,
>   with our spirit.[2]

Lee further states:

> It is indeed inconceivable
> to our natural mind
>   that the almighty God

---

[1] Witness Lee, The Four Major Steps of Christ (Los Angeles: Stream Publishers, 1969), p. 6.

[2] Witness Lee, The Economy of God, (Los Angeles: Stream Publishers, 1968), p. 114.

would one day mingle Himself
with a man.

But this was accomplished
in Jesus Christ,
    and this is the very
    desire of God
    for you and me —
    that He be
    mingled with us.

Do you know what it means
to be a real Christian?
    To be a real Christian
    simply means
    to be mingled with God,
    to be a God-man.[1]

Lee further tells his followers:

What He is, we are;
and what we are, He is.[2]

Before the incarnation,
    God was God
    and man was man,
    but by the incarnation
    God was brought into man,
    and man was brought into God.[3]

He is the God-man
    and we are the God-men . . .
In number we are different,
    but in nature
    we are exactly the same.[4]

---

[1] Witness Lee, The Four Major Steps of Christ (Los Angeles: Stream
Publishers, 1969), p. 7.

[2] Witness Lee, Christianity Versus Religion (Los Angeles: Stream Publishers, 1971), p. 87.

[3] Witness Lee, The Vision of God's Building (Los Angeles: Stream Publishers, 1972), p. 158.

[4] Witness Lee, The All-Inclusive Spirit of Christ (Los Angeles: Stream
Publishers, 1969), p. 103.

Such theology generates disastrous consequences.

1. **God loses His identity.**
   He no longer exists as God, but as a God-mingled mixture. God, in effect, ceases to exist as God.
2. **Man loses his identity.**
   Christ's death is polluted by Witness Lee theology. Man is not redeemed. He is replaced by a mingling process.
3. **Man's normal functions are destroyed.**
   Man, in attempting to be God, assumes the impossible and creates a warped life relationship in the process.

Witness Lee encourages such an abnormal relationship in stating:

> The sisters
>   must forget about their husbands,
> and the brothers
>   must forget about their wives.
> We must forget
>   about our preoccupations
> and see God. . . . [1]

Lee tells his followers that The Local Church is striving to recover the true Church . . . just as it existed about 50 AD.

He sees it emerging from the Protestant Reformation in a five-stage process as follows:

1. Fundamentalism
2. Pentacostalism
3. Evangelism
4. The Deeper Life
5. The Church

The Local Church views itself as the "Church of the Recovery." Anyone remaining in any church denomination is considered blind and needs to join The Local Church for light and life. Lee equates all denominations with Babylon.

---

[1] The Stream, Vol. 7, No. 4, November 1, 1969, p. 11.

Method of Operation

The Local Church gains converts through its conferences and its training programs. Their conferences are held in the summer and run an entire week.

Immediately following the conference comes their indoctrination training program. This is a four-week program in which Witness Lee's theology is introduced. The books, their magazine, The Stream, all concentrate on Lee's writings and thoughts.

The Local Church has in the past put on Gospel Marches. They have marched in groups of 1000 or more in Taipei, in Los Angeles, in New York. They carry huge banners emblazoned with:

The World Is Empty!
You Need Jesus!
Hallelujah!

In uniformed robes to unite them as a group, these marchers sing lustily as they march and attract much attention.

So powerful a hold does The Local Church so grips its members that few leave. Fear and guilt on losing God forever, if they leave, glues them to this movement. The guilt feeling is so strong that some who have left have come crawling back on their hands and knees because they *"experienced the awful judgment of God."*

MEMBERSHIPS and ASSETS

Spiritual Counterfeits Project, Inc. published the data below on some of the current popular religious cults.

Spiritual Counterfeits Project is a nonprofit corporation registered under the laws of the State of California. They publish approximately eight newsletters annually exposing the cults of our day. Their Newsletter and annual SCP Journal are sent to those who request it. They are dependent upon regular financial contributions to cover the cost of these publications and their investigative activities. You may write them at: Spiritual Counterfeits Project, Inc., P.O. Box 4308, Berkeley, California 94704.

GROUP NAME And Leader	Estimated Membership	Estimated Assets
Unification Church Rev. Sun Myung Moon	1,000,000 worldwide 12,000 USA	$219 million
Scientology L. Ron Hubbard	2,000,000 worldwide	$80 million
The Way International Victor Paul Wierwille	40,000 worldwide 60,000 USA	$50 million
Hare Krishna Swami Prabhupada	10,000 worldwide	Multi-million $
Eckankar Darwin Gross	2,000 worldwide 50,000 USA	Multi-million $
The Children of God Moses Berg	5,000 worldwide	$2 million
The Church Universal and Triumphant (Summit Lighthouse) Elizabeth Clare Prophet	5,000 USA	Multi-million $
EST Werner Erhard	150,000 USA	$50 million
Transcendental Meditation Maharishi Mahesh Yogi	1,000,000 USA	$200 million

Maharishi Mahesh Yogi, founder of Transcendental Meditation (TM).

TRANSCENDENTAL MEDITATION (TM)

Background

TM was founded in 1959 in California by Maharishi Mahesh Yogi. Maharishi was formerly a pupil of Guru Dev, who was a leader of a Hindu sect in India. Although claiming to be non-religious, this group is undoubtedly basically Hindu.

Beliefs

The purpose of life is happiness sought through an endless cycle of incarnations and reincarnations.

God is the impersonal *"Creative Intelligence."*

"Seeking to discover who we are" transforms us into *"bliss consciousness."* *"Bliss consciousness"* is only attained through the seven steps of transcendental meditation. This is accomplished by reciting endlessly a liturgy called the **mantra.**

Mantras represent chants to Hindu deities.

Method of Operation

TM offers free introductory lectures, but full courses run about $125 per adult. It is estimated that there are 30,000 initiates in the U.S. each month. A TM University is in Fairfield, Iowa. TM strives for government endorsement and incorporation into classes.

THE UNIFICATION CHURCH

Background

The Unification Church was founded by Sun Myung Moon in Korea in 1954, and established in the United States in 1958. Moon was born in Korea in 1920. His family was Presbyterian. He studied electrical engineering in Japan. In 1936 he claims he had a vision in which Jesus told him "*to carry out my undone task.*"

He began preaching and developed a theological system he called "*The Divine Principle.*" In 1948 he was excommunicated by the Presbyterian Church. In May, 1954 he began the Holy Spirit Association for the Unification of World Christianity. His first wife left him. In 1960 he remarried a very young Korean woman named Hak-Ja Han.

By 1958 he had established a beachhead in Japan and the United States and finally in Europe in the 1960's. The Unification Church grew rapidly once he moved his headquarters to the United States in 1973. Moon is a wealthy businessman and claims about 2 million followers world-wide.

Beliefs

God is single, not triune. Jesus Christ did not fulfill His mission. Sun Myung Moon is the true saviour of the world and the world should unite around him. Jesus Christ is not God. Jesus was a man who perfectly understood what God wanted, and did it.

Jesus is not going to return—but Korea is the Third Israel, from which will come the Lord of the Second Coming. His followers believe Moon is that Lord! Mankind shall become one united family centered around the event of the Second Coming as propagated by Moon. Founder Moon is sinless. Members who have experienced Moon's *"blessing"* can produce a sinless generation (Unification Church 120 Day Training Manual, pgs. 40, 42).

Method of Operation

Moon lives with his wife and eight children in an $8 million, Barrytown, New York estate. This also houses his seminary. "Moonies," as Moon followers are called, live hectic, marginal lives in crowded facilities. Getting new converts is the major thrust of The Unification Church. Followers are indoctrinated with the theology that they cannot reach the kingdom of heaven until they have at least three converts.

The usual technique is to invite friends to a weekend conference. Here the visitor is subjected to a very tight schedule. There is no free time to be alone. The visitor is surrounded with enthusiasm, apparent love, and much attention.

Disillusioned young people become attracted to this window-dressing attention, not realizing the sinister seduction that is taking place. They are invited to a seven-day seminar and then, later, a 21-day training program where intense brainwashing *"converts"* the visitor.

Generally *"trainees"* are brought to the Unification camp in the middle of the night, down a winding, dark road. By this time many have fallen asleep and when they arrive are completely disoriented. Men and women are separated and placed in individual dormitories.

A regulated training schedule is followed. The leader is looked on as the *"parent."* This vertical relationship is encouraged. Horizontal-type relationships with those around you are frowned upon.

Moon $8 Million estate in Barrytown, New York.

(Left) Moonies are trained to raise money using patriotic theme.
(Right) A regulated training schedule leaves little free time.

Moonies are trained to raise money, by selling candy, flowers, anything. A typical Moonie can bring in from $100 to $500 a day.

Each Sunday morning at 5 AM, Moonies assemble and hold a *"pledge"* service. The group begins by bowing down three times to the heavenly Father and the True Parents (Moon and Wife).

Moonies believe it is permissible to lie. They call it *"Heavenly Deception,"* and use it particularly when fund raising. Moon says:

> *If you tell a lie to make a person better,*
> *then that is not sin . . .*
> *Even God tells lies very often.*
>   (Master Speaks, March 16, 1972, p. 11)

Moon has a membership of about one-half million followers in his Unification Church. In the United States there are about 7000 hard core members and another 30,000 loosely adhering to the church.

The Unification Church operates under many front organizations which include:

International Re-education Foundation
High School International Family Association
International Cultural Foundation
DC Striders Track Club
International Federation for Victory over Communism
World Freedom Institute
One World Crusade
American Youth for a Just Peace
Collegiate Association for the Research of Principles (CARP)

Moon, using *"Heavenly Deception"* often invites government officials and community leaders to special dinners and receptions. Moon also plays up such worthy causes as patriotism and anti-communism to achieve his own ulterior ends.

UNITY and UNITY SCHOOL OF CHRISTIANITY

Background

Unity was founded by Myrtle and Charles Fillmore in the 1880's. Myrtle Fillmore had suffered with both tuberculosis and malaria from childhood. In 1886 Myrtle and her husband attended a lecture given by Dr. Eugene B. Weeks of the Illinois Metaphysical College. The College had connections with Mary Baker Eddy and Christian Science.

One phrase impressed Myrtle Fillmore from the Week's lecture: *"I am a child of God and therefore I do not inherit sickness."* She no longer thought of herself as an invalid and in two years claimed healing. She wrote her story in the book, How I Found Health.

Her husband had also been a cripple from an early age. He applied his wife's new theology of healing and claimed that his chronic pains ceased and his leg lengthened and he was able to get rid of the steel extention he had worn since a child. Desirous of sharing their new faith, in 1889 they published their new magazine, Modern Thought.

In this publication they wrote: *"We see the good in all religions and we want everyone to feel free to find the Truth for himself wherever he may be led to find it."* In 1891, they adopted for their religion the name of **UNITY**.

Beliefs

In adopting their new name they issued their statement of principle:

> *"Unity of the soul with God, unity of all life, unity of all religions, unity of the spirit, soul and body; unity of all men in the heart of truth."*

Unity has taken elements of Christian Science (healing), of Rosicrucianism (cosmic unity), of Quakerism (inner light), and of Spiritism (the astral self).

Unity does not accept the Bible as Divine Revelation. They do not accept Jesus as God but simply as a man who was good. Jesus made no real atonement at Calvary, according to Unity, but simply demonstrated the power of mind over matter. Christ's resurrection was not a miracle but thought control.

Unity also believes in the doctrine of reincarnation. Article 22 of their Statement of Faith reveals:

> "We believe that the dissolution of spirit, soul, and body—caused by death—is annulled by rebirth of the same spirit and soul in another body here on earth."

Reincarnation is not Scriptural. See Hebrews 9:27, Romans 5:12, 2 Corinthians 5:8.

Method of Operation

Unity grew rapidly under the guidance of Fillmore's two sons, Lowell and Rickert. Unity has one of the largest printing plants in the Midwest. They publish top quality devotional-type material which includes Unity and Daily Word. It has been estimated that they publish more than 100 books and booklets annually and over 100 million pieces of literature. Their mail averages about 10,000 letters each day and they receive over 750,000 requests for prayer each year.

They have a correspondence school at Unity Village. These impressive headquarters are located on a 1200-acre site near Lee's Summit, Missouri. Lee's Summit is a suburb of Kansas City. Unity has an estimated following of over a million members. It has been termed the largest mail order religious concern in the world.

THE WAY, INTERNATIONAL

Background

Victor Paul Wierwille had grown up in fundamentalist circles. In his late fifties, he became a minister in the Evangelical and Reformed Church (now the United Church of Christ). He was born in 1917.

Wierwille was a graduate of Princeton Theological Seminary. He received a Masters degree in Practical Theology. He was frustrated because the ministry was not moving fast enough for him. He sought a scheme that would build a dynamic ministry based on the abundant life. He became obsessed with the verse in John 10:10:

I am come
that they might have life,
and that they might have it
more abundantly.

This verse is rich in Scriptural truth, but Wierwille ignored basic foundational doctrines of the Bible and put together his own patchwork theology centered on abundant living. He called his Bible study course, "Power for Abundant Living." He cloaked it in familiar evangelical vocabulary and began his heretical ministry.

While The Way ministry is claimed to have begun in 1942, Wierwille's cult only began to experience real growth when it moved its headquarters to New Knoxville, Ohio in 1968. Wierwille was able to capitalize on the nondiscriminating religious interests of many of the growing Jesus Movements at that time. He won them through his *"Rock of Ages Festival"* held annually.

In 1975, Wierwille opened The Way College in Emporia, Kansas with some 400 students.

Beliefs

Victor Paul Wierwille, promotes The Way ministry with a strange theology which includes the statement:

Jesus Christ is not God!
Jesus Christ was not with God
*   in the beginning.*

Wierwille is definitely against both the doctrine of the Trinity and any teaching that places Jesus Christ on the same level as God. He claims the Trinity is pagan and was created by the Roman emperor Constantine.

Wierwille does not accept the Holy Spirit as part of the Trinity. The Holy Spirit, in The Way theology, is just another convenient name for God. Wierwille is big on capitalized letters. When the Holy Spirit refers to God it is capitalized! Christians, Wierwille claims, are not filled with the Holy Spirit. He sees them filled with the holy spirit (small *h* and small *s*). Wierwille says that there is one gift but nine *"manifestations"* of that one gift. They include: speaking in tongues, prophecy and healing. While every person has these gifts, Wierwille says they have not learned to use them.

Wierwille has conveniently worked out a purely mechanical method so that everyone in The Way movement can speak in tongues. In Session 12 of the Power for Abundant Living class, devotees are coached on how to speak in tongues. Wierwille has a *"how-to-do-it"* book in which he outlines four steps leading up to the tongues experience. Wierwille places great emphasis on the necessity of speaking in tongues and many of his followers speak in tongues for hours each day.

The Way theology emphasizes that salvation is merely a legal transaction secured by the death and resurrection of Christ. Salvation, according to Wierwille, can only be experienced by gaining the right knowledge. And what is that *"right"* knowledge? It is through the various Bible study courses of The Way.

Victor Paul Wierwille often traveled by motorcycle in early days to win converts. Above is the Way Tree symbol used to develop a highly organized religious following.

Method of Operation

Victor Paul Wierwille has devised an effective way to win converts to The Way. **Phase One** is to deprogram the individual from any Biblical concepts that are counter to The Way theology. Their historic Christian faith is shredded by Wierwille's book, *"Jesus Christ is NOT God."*

After pulling away this keystone of faith, Wierwille then begins **Phase Two.** Mind manipulation begins with his heavy emphasis on "renewing of the mind." The Way teaches:

> *By conditioning our minds*
> *through a renewal of the mind process,*
> *we can correct*
> *imperfect chains or patterns*
> *in the brain.*
>
> (Walter J. Cummins, *"The Mind of the Believer,"*
> *The Way* magazine, July/August, 1974, pp. 10, 11.)

On the surface this may appear perfectly enlightening and spiritual. But it must be remembered that this conditioning of the mind is done through The Way patchwork theology which warps the mind into the mold of this cult.

Parents soon see the behavior of their children changing. The Way mind molding technique soon colors the devotee's thinking and his actions. He becomes brainwashed into Wierwille "theology."

The Way followers become followers of a deadly legalism, slaves of the law . . . abandoning God's grace through His Son Jesus Christ! In effect, they are robots . . . programmed to respond according to a pre-set plan.

The Way is highly organized. Their organization is called The Way Tree. The roots are the International Headquarters in New Knoxville, Ohio; the trunk is made up of the national organizations; the limb, the state organizations; the branch, the city organizations and the twig, the local fellowship. Some have estimated that there are about 25,000 followers in about 1800 "twig" fellowships.[1]

They claim they are not a church. They are aggressive in door-to-door canvassing. Word Over The World Ambassadors (WOW) are young people who enlist for one year to be sent wherever The Way wants them to win converts. At least 1000 such Ambassadors are sent out annually. They find part-time work and support themselves. New converts are charged $85 for the 12-session Wierwille "Power for Abundant Living" video-tape course.

The Way has its own bookstore. They produce radio and television programming. They have their own press . . . The American Christian Press. They are engaged in politics: Christian Political Alliance (CPA). They have their own total

---

[1] Jack Sparks, The Mind Benders (Nashville: Thomas Nelson, Inc., 1977), p. 200.

fitness program. They call it TFI, Total Fitness Institute. They are now in 30 countries and their course is translated into Spanish, French and German.

When one becomes a member of The Way Corps program he finds his time rigidly structured. Each member must keep a daily, hour-by-hour record of exactly how he spends his time. The form he fills out is called: "*Redeemed Time Analysis.*" Columns start at 5:00 AM and go to midnight.

Security is The Way theme, like many other cult groups. It leaves the young person free of making any decisions. His time is programmed. His work is programmed. Even how much toilet paper he uses is programmed! One former Way follower states:

> The Group's control extended
> to everyday necessities.
> They explained:
>   It's not love
>   to use too much toilet paper.
> We were made
>   to feel bad
>   for using
>   too much toilet paper.
> Your mind is always
>   geared and directed.
> You no longer
>   think for yourself.
> You think
>   what you are told
>   to think.[1]

The Way is definitely seeking to win young people who will be tomorrow's leaders of the world. They have a goal of sending out 6000 College Ambassadors to infiltrate all the major campuses in the United States.

---

[1] Ronald Enroth, Youth Brainwashing, and the Extremist Cults (Grand Rapids: Zondervan Publishing House, 1977), p. 131.

Use this ORDER FORM to order additional copies of

SATAN'S ANGELS EXPOSED

by Salem Kirban

You will want to give **SATAN'S ANGELS EXPOSED** to your loved ones and friends.

An excellent book to give to those who want to know how their world is changing and want to be prepared for the future . . . the next 10 years . . . and eternity!

PRICES

**SAVE $$$$
BUY IN BULK!**

Single copy: $4.95
3 copies $12.00 (You save $2.85)
5 copies $18.75 (You save $6.00)
10 copies $32.50 (You save $17.00)
25 copies $75.00 (You save $48.75)

WE PAY POSTAGE!

ORDER FORM

SALEM KIRBAN, Inc.
Mason's Mill Business Park
Huntingdon Valley, Penna. 19006 U.S.A.

Enclosd find $ _____ **for** _____ **copies of**
SATAN'S ANGELS EXPOSED by Salem Kirban.

Ship postage paid to:

Mr.
Mrs.
Name Miss _____
(Please PRINT)

Address _____

City _____

State _____ Zip Code _____

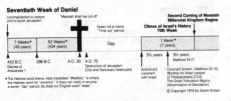

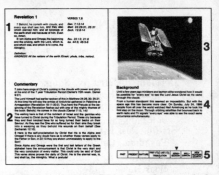

RECOMMENDED READING

You may order these books direct from your local bookstore.

DeHaan, Richard W. *Satan, Satanism and Witchcraft.* Grand Rapids: Zondervan Publishing House, 1972.

Enroth, Ronald. *Youth Brainwashing, and the Extremist Cults.* Grand Rapids: Zondervan Publishing House, 1977.

Griffin, Des. *Fourth Reich of the Rich.* Emissary Publications, P.O. Box 642, South Pasadena, California 91030, 1978.

Gruss, Edmond C. *Cults and the Occult in the Age of aquarius.* Grand Rapids: Baker Book House, 1974.

Hoekema, Anthony A. *The Four Major Cults* (Christian Science, Jehovah's Witnesses, Mormonism, Seventh-day Adventism. Grand Rapids: William B. Eerdmans Publishing Company, 1963.

Martin, Walter R. *The Kingdom of the Cults.* Minneapolis: Bethany Fellowship, 1965.

Means, Pat. *The Mystical Maze.* California: Campus Crusade for Christ, 1976.

Miller, William M. A. *Christian's Response to Islam.* Phillipsburg, New Jersey: Presbyterian and Reformed Publishing Company, 1979.

Pentecost, J. Dwight. *Your Adversary The Devil.* Grand Rapids: Zondervan, 1969.

Sparks, Jack. *The Mind Benders.* Nashville: Thomas Nelson, Inc., 1977.

Unger, Merrill F. *Biblical Demonology.* Wheaton, Illinois: Scripture Press Publications, 1952.

BOOKS by SALEM KIRBAN on the Four Major Cults

SALEM KIRBAN PRESENTS

JEHOVAH'S WITNESSES

JEHOVAH'S WITNESSES

How is it possible for this group to print 50,000 books a day in their Brooklyn Headquarters? How has the Watchtower magazine catapulted Jehovah's Witnesses into the fastest growing cult today? Why did Mrs. Russell ask for a divorce? Why did Judge Rutherford go to jail? What is each member of their congregation required to do? Who are their 144,000? Why is the date 1914 so important to them?

SALEM KIRBAN PRESENTS

MORMONISM

MORMONISM

Who are those young men with that well-scrubbed look who knock on doors? Why do they do it? Why do they pay their own way as Mormon missionaries? What strange findings that first began with eight barges and an ocean trip gave birth to an unusual cult? Why did they build a $2 million vault in the Granite Mountains near Salt Lake City? What state in the United States will possess the "keys to the world power?"

SALEM KIRBAN PRESENTS

CHRISTIAN SCIENCE

Mary Baker Eddy

CHRISTIAN SCIENCE

Why do Christian Scientists owe their origin to a horse? Who was Phineas Quimby and why do Christian Scientists hate to hear his name mentioned? What tragedies occurred in Mary Baker Eddy's life that triggered her search for a new religion? Why did Dr. Noyes remove Mary Baker Eddy's husband's heart and show it to her in her own living room? How vast is the Christian Science empire today?

SALEM KIRBAN PRESENTS

ARMSTRONG'S CHURCH OF GOD

THE PLAIN TRUTH ABOUT THE PLAIN TRUTH

ARMSTRONG'S CHURCH OF GOD

Why is Herbert W. Armstrong's cult considered the most deceptive of all cults? Why do even Christians fall into the snare set by the Armstrong trap? Why is the Plain Truth simply *not* the Plain Truth? What importance did the "neighbor next door" have to do with this strange cult? What is the secret of Armstrong's growth? How is this operation financed? How does it win and hold converts? What promises does it take from Israel?